The 1980s

Jim Durrant is appointed Sales Director

    Royal Wedding—HRH Prince Charles and Lady Diana Spencer

Wiley acquires Heyden journals

Wiley Ltd adds the Booth Rooms to its premises (1982)

Adrian Higham moves to New York office as Vice President, International Group (1982)

Charlie Stoll is acting Managing Director of Wiley Ltd (1982/3)

Mike Foyle is appointed Managing Director in 1983

John Wilde is appointed Sales & Marketing Director

The Duke of Richmond joins the board of Wiley Ltd as Deputy Chairman in 1984

First fax machines come to Wiley

Wiley extends Corn Exchange building into back of the old Granada Cinema (1984)

Sales exceed £10 million (FY83)

    Thames flood barrier completed

    Henry VIII's ship, the *Mary Rose*, is raised

Apollo digital production system introduced

Sales exceed £15 million (FY84)

Jim Durrant retires (1985)

Harry Newman retires (1985)

Tim Davies joins as Finance Director (1986)

Peter Ferris becomes Systems and Distribution Director

Wiley Ltd launches first interactive video disk

    Launch of Sinclair C5

In 1987 ...

Jamie Cameron leaves Wiley

John Jarvis appointed Editorial Director

Mark Bide joins as Production Director

Ruth McMullin is appointed Chief Executive Officer of Wiley Inc. to succeed Andy Neilly

Production Division moves into Stocklund House (1987)

    Hurricane hits Southern England

THIRTY YEARS IN CHICHESTER

THIRTY YEARS IN CHICHESTER
A Celebration

*being a history of John Wiley & Sons Ltd
from the company's move to Chichester in 1967
until the present day*

JOHN WILEY & SONS

CHICHESTER • NEW YORK • WEINHEIM • BRISBANE • SINGAPORE • TORONTO

Copyright © 1997 by John Wiley & Sons Ltd,
Baffins Lane, Chichester,
West Sussex PO19 1UD, England

National 01243 779777
International (+44) 1243 779777
e-mail (for orders and customer service enquiries):
cs-books@wiley.co.uk
Visit out Home Page on http://www.wiley.co.uk
or http://www.wiley.com

All Rights Reserved. No part of this publication may be reproduced, stored in a retrieval system, or transmitted, in any form or by any means, electronic, mechanical, photocopying, recording, scanning or otherwise, except under the terms of the Copyright, Designs and Patents Act 1988 or under the terms of a licence issued by the Copyright Licensing Agency, 90 Tottenham Court Road, London, UK W1P 9HE, without the permission in writing of the publisher.

Other Wiley Editorial Offices

John Wiley & Sons, Inc., 605 Third Avenue,
New York, NY 10158-0012, USA

Wiley-VCH Verlag GmbH, Papelallee 3,
D-69469 Weinheim, Germany

Jacaranda Wiley Ltd, 33 Park Road, Milton,
Queensland 4064, Australia

John Wiley & Sons (Asia) Pte Ltd, 2 Clementi Loop #02-01,
Jin Xing Distripark, Singapore 129809

John Wiley & Sons (Canada) Ltd, 22 Worcester Road,
Rexdale, Ontario M9W 1L1, Canada

ISBN 0-471-97656-3

Typeset in 11/13 pt Garamond by BookEns Ltd, Royston, Hertfordshire
Printed and bound in Great Britain by Bookcraft (Bath) Ltd, Midsomer Norton, Somerset
This book is printed on acid-free paper responsibly manufactured from sustainable forestry, for which at least two trees are planted for each one used for paper production.

Contents

Acknowledgements	vi
Foreword	vii
Preface	ix
Introduction—The End of the Beginning	xiii
Setting the Scene	1
Chapter 1 The Move	25
Chapter 2 Wiley in the 1970s	65
Chapter 3 Selling and Marketing Around the World	71
Chapter 4 Information Technology at Wiley, 1967–1997	97
Chapter 5 The 1980s	107
Chapter 6 Editorial and Production	117
Chapter 7 Servicing Our Customers	135
Chapter 8 The 1990s	149
Chapter 9 Special Occasions	163
Chapter 10 Buildings1	175
Chapter 11 The Social Calendar	183
Chapter 12 Memorable Communications	213
Afterword	225

Acknowledgements

OUR THANKS to all those who have contributed articles and photographs to this book, and to our publishing committee—Gordon Barclay, Mike Coombs, Karin Davies, Peter Ferris, Shirley Howard, Bob Long, Angela Poulter, Graham Russel, Monica Twine and Verity Waite. Special thanks to Graham for managing the production, to Peter for providing the timeline, and to Verity for putting the material together and overseeing the entire project.

Thanks also to the many people who sent in material which we were unable to use (for reasons of space or in some cases, decency!), and to those who kindly lent their back issues of *Grapevine* and *Wiley World*, particularly Clare Chaplin who had lovingly kept every issue of both. These were invaluable in helping us to track the major events of the 1980s and 1990s.

We should also like to thank the *Chichester Observer* for giving us their permission to use several articles and advertisements published during the 1960s.

Finally, for contributing photographs and graphics, thanks to:

Karin Davies	Smyth Pollock
Jim Dicks	Gaynor Redvers-Mutton
Geoff Farrell	Mike Shardlow
Peter Ferris	Monica Twine
Mike Foyle	Stefan Usansky
Ronnie Gorlin	Verity Waite
Alan Hawes	Deanna Waldron
Wendy Hudlass	Liz Warden
Peter Marriage	Sheila Woodrow

Foreword

His Grace the tenth Duke of Richmond

THIS YEAR sees for me two important local anniversaries, very different from one another and yet closely connected with me personally.

As current Chairman of John Wiley and Sons Ltd I am delighted to participate in the celebrations of Wiley's 30 years in Chichester, a city with which my family has had a close association for over 250 years.

As the tenth Duke of Richmond I am pleased this year to be celebrating the purchase by my ancestor, first Duke of Richmond, son of King Charles II, of a little hunting box, later called Goodwood House, exactly 300 years ago.

I wonder what the first Duke of Richmond would have thought of the books now produced by Wiley and the process of doing so, not least the advanced technology which goes into it! In particular he would surely have been amazed at the significant contribution made to the local economy by Wiley employing locally some 400 staff and by Goodwood employing some 300.

The impact of Wiley's presence in the locality has now reached a very important level. Wiley are now the largest employers in Chichester city, but even more than that because of the quality and skills of the people employed by them the contribution to the local economy in terms of the total salary bill must be very much the largest in the city. For the same reasons the staff make a significant input to many of the activities of the city, not least to educational and cultural pursuits.

The company itself directly contributes to these pursuits, such as the Festival Theatre and the Festivities, and provides hospitality through Goodwood Races and Goodwood Festival of Speed!

Many American, German and other foreigners increasingly visit Chichester through Wiley, and the city benefits both culturally and economically from its association with them. But even more so the increasingly international nature of the business itself and the foreign exchange it generates is not only important to Chichester but to Britain and Europe as a whole.

Today Chichester without Wiley would not only be unthinkable but in many ways disastrous! Indeed I know how much the local councils, county, district and city, value the presence of Wiley in Chichester and hope for many years to come it will remain there, even if it should outgrow its present premises!

But also to me and my family, the presence of Wiley in the local scene is important, for not only Goodwood but the whole local community needs prosperous, growing firms of high quality and standards.

I hope that my grandson in 30 years' time (the twelfth Duke—we hope—now aged 2) will be able to congratulate Wiley on their continued presence and even greater prosperity!

Preface

A PUBLISHING SUCCESS STORY IN WEST SUSSEX

Brad Wiley and Brad Wiley II

WE CONSIDER it an honor to contribute some prefatory remarks to the reminiscences and reflections collected here to celebrate John Wiley & Sons Ltd's 30 years' residence in the county seat, cathedral and market town of Chichester, West Sussex.

This celebration here in the spring of 1997 in our understanding is not to apotheosize the story of Baffins Lane the catalytic agent in the story the post-World War II story of Wiley the global publisher. That episode, rich and heroic a publishing narrative though it may be, will find another time for the telling and signification.

To us the achievement to be remarked upon and celebrated here is the success of what was, after all at the time of its initiation, a pioneering and unorthodoxically experimental decision to move the firm out of London to a place with no previous history of supporting the technical and cultural needs of an extremely specialized craft business, scientific and technical publishing. In short, moving to Chichester was, as we look back from this summer 30 years later, a remarkably successful gamble.

Taking us back to the mid-1960s, what the elder of us recollects is a successful fledgling of the parent John Wiley & Sons, a six-year-old subsidiary importing and selling New York titles and journals, beginning to develop its own UK and Europe-based authors and publishing programs, and operating out of (for the standards of the industry in those days) extremely dear real estate in Glen House, Victoria.

We recollect that Wiley and Chichester have to thank the new generation of operating managers attracted to the growing London business, the likes of Jamie Cameron, Mike Colenso, Mike Coombs, Jim Durrant, and Ove Steentoft, and others, with the support of parent company senior officers, for provoking the initiative to leave expensive and labor market unstable London for what must have appeared in those times to be deepest rural England, well on the south side of the South Downs.

Then Managing Director, Ron Watson, an accomplished chemistry editor, was himself of the generation that understood London as the cultural center of the craft and trade of scientific and technical publishing. But once inspired by the views of his younger colleagues and with encouragement from the parent company, Mr Watson initiated the site exploration exercise by drawing on a map a circle around the city radius 50 miles and then mandating pursuit of a location outside this circle commonly perceived as beyond the commuting range between city center and its suburbs. Wiley Ltd's management wanted, and the parent company supported, any ties between the staff and the vagaries of the London labor environment virtually severed. We also think that, while Chichester ultimately became the firm's exurban destination, Watson and his colleagues explored and considered locations as far away as Bath.

Chichester in 1967, one of us recollects, was a far more rural place both materially and spiritually than the younger generation can imagine possible. Wiley Ltd's management itself knew at the time it would have to judge correctly whether such a pastoral environment and culture could recruit and sustain employees with the skills and outlook required to sustain a "sophisticated" enterprise as scientific and technical publishing. This concern was equally embraced by the emigrating editorial and marketing staff, who wondered what kind of a lifestyle lay in store for them once they abandoned the great cosmopolis that was so much a part of their definition of the appropriate publishing milieu.

All's well that ends well: in 1967 Chichester itself was in the first stage of its own "urban renewal" project, refitting for commercial use a number of the Georgian buildings inside the city wall. The Wiley pioneer emigrants found an interesting, essentially abandoned building in Baffins Lane, the pigeons and starlings, along with their coprilitic baggage, were encouraged to surrender the Corn Exchange with its aura of dust and cereals, and defer to the establishment of publishing enterprise in those historic quarters. Exurban staff settled into the life and pace of the West Sussex community with evident enthusiasm; and new local employees contributed significantly to the success of the move as co-creators of the publishing success story that describes this firm now, John Wiley & Sons Ltd, standing itself alone a generation and a half later, a major scientific, technical and medical house on the roster of worldwide publishers in these fields today.

Retrospectively it might seem inevitable that the outcome of that 1965 decision to move out of London would eventuate in an enterprise publishing today 150 journals and 400 new titles a year for the global market, with a staff of some 375 highly professional souls located in three different buildings up and down East and West Streets and in Bognor Regis, with a sales force stretched over the continents of Asia, Africa and Europe. Perhaps it was inevitable, and perhaps not.

However, what we are confident of identifying as determining is that it has been the working and living atmosphere in and around Chichester, West Sussex that has enabled Wiley Ltd to become what we describe it as being in the sentences above. What this firm has achieved in the past thirty years would likely not have happened in the London milieu post-1967.

Necessary but not sufficient describes Chichester the place as catalyst to the success of the enterprise here over the decades. To complete the equation we must also recognize the people who participated in the pioneering story we are celebrating here, the bold decision makers who took the risk there in 1967 to uproot themselves from their traditional publishers' habitat and move, and since then the generation and a half of publishing professionals in the firm here whose dedication, day upon week, career by career, title by title, serial by serial, account by account, has made the enterprise what we see it as today. Our congratulations go to each of them for what they have contributed to the sum of the enterprise here, today, 1997.

And as to whether it is this intelligent, skilled and dedicated publishing team that creates the special publishing culture at Wiley Ltd in Chichester or whether it is the special ambience life has in West Sussex that is more determinant of the success of what has been achieved here in the last thirty years, we propose that we reserve the outcome of that discussion for the next celebration of John Wiley & Sons Ltd in this old town 10 or 20 years hence.

W. Bradford Wiley
DIRECTOR EMERITUS

Bradford Wiley II
CHAIRMAN OF THE BOARD

Introduction—The End of the Beginning

John Jarvis

THERE HAVE been many sigificant events in Wiley's 190-year history, but a milestone referred to in this year's annual report has a particular relevance to the story we recall and celebrate in this volume.

For the first time in its history, US territory sales of Wiley publications in 1997/98 will be exceeded by sales made throughout the rest of the world. This is not, of course, solely the result of Wiley Ltd's activity but also that of our International Development Group, Wiley Canada and the newly acquired Wiley-VCH Verlag GmbH in Germany. In the pages that follow, however, you will read our former Chairman's account of the establishment in 1960 of what has become Wiley's largest overseas enterprise—the London-based UK subsidiary and its subsequent relocation to Chichester in the summer of 1967. During the intervening 30 years, the development of the Chichester operation has closely influenced the growth of the corporation's sales outside the USA, resulting in this year's milestone geographic sales distribution.

Such a sales statistic is primarily a testament to the vision and perseverance of those who sought new markets and authors in Europe more than 30 years ago, but it is in fact only one indicator of Chichester's contribution within Wiley and does not creditably describe the year-on-year steady progress of a successful business and those who have participated in it. We have attempted here to present an eclectic account of this development rather than a comprehensive historic record, with a collection of reminiscences that capture much of the attitude and culture that have underpinned our development and which hopefully continue to the present day and beyond.

Successful subsidiaries require firm but tolerant parent organisations who realise, rather like twentieth-century Britain finally did, that successful global empires require more than the dissemination of one culture around the world if they are to evolve into a sustainable commonwealth of self-confident yet interdependent parts. Wiley, I believe, is coming close to creating that commonwealth, and in times of unparalleled technological change the company will require all the self-confidence it can muster. Reading these contributions suggests that a combination of self-confidence and pragmatism has been a good one for achieving success in the somewhat special business environment afforded to Wiley by Chichester, and I gladly accept the responsibility to nurture what I inherited from my predecessors in order to sustain our achievements.

It is no surprise to me that several contributors here reflect rather wistfully on the past 30 years. The past is always more certain than the future, particularly such an unpredictable future, but here my confidence in securing it for us stems from the very predictability of my colleagues' constancy both in professional performance and personal loyalty to the company.

On behalf of all Wiley Ltd staff, I gratefully thank our parent organisation for its confidence and trust in allowing us to develop; and I warmly thank all Wiley Ltd staff (past and present) who have enabled us to reach this significant anniversary, which one day will surely be seen as only the end of the beginning of this Chichester story.

Setting the Scene

EXCERPT FROM A MEMOIR BEING PREPARED
FOR PUBLICATION BY W. BRADFORD WILEY
IN COLLABORATION WITH HIS SON
PETER BOOTH WILEY

ONE OF my major assignments in the years after World War II was to lead the charge in the international arena focusing initially on Europe. Wiley had been deeply involved with the British publishing scene from its earliest years. In 1838 John Wiley dispatched his junior partner George Palmer Putnam to England where he opened an office for Wiley & Putnam on Paternoster Row in 1841. Together they arranged to publish American editions of prominent British authors, such as Charles Dickens and John Ruskin. Both Wiley and Putnam insisted on paying royalties to their British authors, an uncommon practice at a time when their principal rivals, such as the Harper brothers, were well-known pirates.

For many, many years the British company of Chapman & Hall distributed our books in England and Europe. This arrangement was made by William Halsted Wiley on a trip to London in 1895. William Halsted was my great grandfather's brother. He was an engineer and was known as the Major because he commanded two artillery companies in the American Civil War. The Major was an internationalist with connections in England and the American correspondent and agent for the British journal *Engineering*. Our books did well enough in England and Europe that Chapman & Hall decided to start its own scientific-technical list. Our combined lists reached some 1,400 titles after World War I. Ten years after the arrangement with Chapman & Hall the Major traveled to Asia setting up agency arrangements with Edward Evans & Sons in Shanghai, the Philippine Education Company in Manila, and Maruzen in Tokyo. We had a similar agency arrangement with the Renouf Publishing Company of Montreal.

During the Industrial Revolution many of the first generation of American scientists were trained in European universities, particularly in Germany after the Franco-Prussian War. Toward the end of the nineteenth century the Major began buying rights to European books, particularly German chemistry books, for translation in the United States. These books helped educate a second generation of American scientists who were trained at home. After World War I the Major continued to buy rights despite the common European practice of charging high prices because we were considered rich Yankees. Springer Verlag was particularly known for this practice. But all in all Wiley's focus at that time was on the domestic market, and international sales and imports were not an important part of the business. Witness the fact that no one in the office was assigned responsibility for international sales until we set up an export division immediately after World War II.

After World War II, the prolonged process by which English became the second language of the world accelerated. This was a surprise to us, perhaps not as much as it was to nonscientific-technical publishers. Interestingly it was somewhat of a shock to the British even though they were still thinking in imperial terms. The emergence of English, in time, led to a new kind of competition in the sci-tech field with European publishers because as books in English began to dominate markets, the European publishers began to publish most of their journals and books, particularly their professional and reference books in English. This began in the 1950s and by the 1970s the Dutch and the Germans were publishing almost all of their journals in English. There was new competition from Germany and even France. The Dutch, of course, had been publishing in English before the war. So the American publishers, who were to become major performers in all these markets, had more competition than they had before although that did not seem to have a negative impact.

There were other events that took place in the postwar period, such as changes in world of education. In the third world, our aid programs, which emphasized building up a country's infrastructure, began to pay for improvements in the recipient countries' educational systems. Lots of students were brought to the United States, mostly graduate students, but some undergraduates, and very slowly the American system of higher education became an important new world standard. The impact of our educational system even extended beyond the developing countries because in the developed countries of Scandinavia, Western Europe, and the United Kingdom, universities were moving away from being elitist institutions. New types of universities, such as the so-called red brick universities in Britain, emerged and became excellent very quickly. There was an increased demand for textbooks also because the traditional tutorial system could not cope with the number of new students. And finally there was the need to rebuild the libraries destroyed during the war. Thus it was inevitable that Wiley should look overseas.

Once we did it was not hard to establish contact with the European and British scientific communities. During the 1930s we had become well-acquainted with the large numbers of outstanding scientific refugees who came to the United States to escape from European fascism and anti-semitism. Some had become our authors; others were close friends. By the time the war ended, this group of scientists had established themselves in the United States and had made important contributions in the research development programs in the biological sciences, chemistry, mathematics, statistics, and physics. After the war some of these scientists chose to return home; others became citizens. At this time our authors and friends in the scientific community urged us to seek direct contact with the returning scientists and their colleagues in England and Europe.

We also began to notice that the sale of foreign rights increased rapidly after World War II. Europeans were eager to learn about the results of our wartime research. So we began to think ahead. We already had the Chapman & Hall relationship. McGraw Hill had a company in England tied to their magazine publishing, and Van Nostrand had a small office in London. We informed Chapman & Hall that as of a certain date, probably in the late 1940s, we were planning to deal directly with the European market from New York. Soon after, Jack McDougall, the managing director of Chapman & Hall, came to New York. He was a wonderful Scot, a charming man, an intellectual, something of a heavy drinker, but not a sci-tech publisher. His charming American wife, Mary, was the daughter of a senior officer at one of the larger banks in New York. One of Jack's principal responsibilities was to deal with Evelyn Waugh, the famous British author, who was published by Chapman & Hall. In the course of our meeting we talked about various things, but Jack forgot to tell us that Chapman & Hall now belonged to Methuen & Company.

Our next visit was from Sir Stanley Unwin, head of Allen and Unwin, the London publishing house. We took him to lunch at the Players Club where he very quickly presented his request for distribution rights for Wiley books in Europe and the United Kingdom. We thanked him and said it was our intention as soon as possible to open a subsidiary in London with the initial intent of distributing our books not only in the United Kingdom, but throughout Europe and Scandinavia. Our second objective was to set up a publishing house that would publish books, either original or in translation, in English. It was from Sir Stanley that we learned that Methuen had bought Chapman & Hall.

We needed to do something better than we were doing. We were getting some sales out of the United States International Book Association, which had a couple of employees working out of an office in Amsterdam. This was a jointly owned distribution system involving several companies, which was set up in 1948 with the permission of the US government. The government had decided to waive the fair trade laws banning price fixing and special discounts so as to encourage US exports. The USIBA sold primarily sci-tech books, but all in all it did not work that well. In France, for example, books were sent to bookstores, but it was hard to collect from many accounts. Credit was being extended to those who hardly qualified, and bookstore owners were having a hard time getting their hands on dollars to pay their bills. It often took as much as three months to acquire dollars.

We decided that we would set up an import and distribution company in England because Chapman & Hall was really not handling our account very well. The decisions about England and Europe were made in early 1948. As had happened before in my career, I happened to be the right Wiley officer in the right place at the right time. By that time I was Vice President, and I was assigned the responsibility of making an exploratory trip to Europe. I then communicated at length by mail and phone with a host of our authors who had personal connections through professional societies or through European scientists who worked in the United States with scientists in Europe. I got a mountain of information with introductions to here, there, and everywhere, even to the great Brown Boveri Company, the General Electric of Switzerland. I laid out an itinerary including plans for visits with booksellers in Paris, Copenhagen, Zurich, Amsterdam, Stockholm and Oslo. W.O. Wiley, our chairman, and Ed Hamilton, our president, had visited London twice in the 1930s to meet with Chapman & Hall, but no Wiley employee had ever visited any of the English or European booksellers. Somewhere along the way I was told my wife Esther should accompany me. Esto was not very happy over the prospect of being away from home for about ten weeks. Air travel was still extremely limited at that time, typically available only for VIPs making short trips. We would be traveling by ship and were leaving three young Wiley's at home. We hired a nurse-housekeeper to take care of the children, which solved the problem.

Off we went sailing on the *Queen Mary*. It was a great adventure because neither of us had crossed the Atlantic before. The *Queen Mary* had recently been overhauled and returned to transatlantic service after serving as a troop transport during the war. We made a number of acquaintances on board, but, of course, never saw them again. Among the passengers were Mr and Mrs Jose Ferrer, Errol Flynn and his current wife, Ruth Gordon, Lord Beaverbrook, and Mr and Mrs Winston Churchill. Churchill spent the entire passage in a special suite assigned to them, emerging only after midnight to walk the enclosed deck. Mrs Churchill joined the large number of passengers who vigorously walked the deck at least once and sometimes twice a day. With us we took nylon stockings and tin smoked hams because the food situation in England was pretty grim, and nylons had just come on the market.

The *Queen Mary* arrived in the English Channel in midafternoon headed for a stopover at Cherbourg prior to docking in Southampton the next day. About dinner time, the ship began to pitch and roll, a common occurrence in the Channel. Esther and I were sitting in the cocktail lounge in chairs that were anchored to the deck. Some of the people sitting around us were less fortunate, and many of them went over backwards in the increasingly violent action of the ship. At dinner that evening we found the first class restaurant thinly populated. Sideboards were up on the tables, and the table cloth dampened to prevent plates from sliding back and forth. We ate well as usual and were advised after dinner to return to our stateroom as a matter of safety. Most of the night was quite wild, but we felt secure because the sideboards on our bunks were high enough to prevent us from rolling onto the floor. The next morning the restaurant was even more thinly populated.

In the morning we entered Cherbourg slowly because the harbor was still partially obstructed by the hulks of ships sunk during the war. We finally reached Southampton very late in the evening where the courier who was to meet us did not catch up with us until we reached our hotel in London. We stayed in Grosvenor House, that huge hotel on the south end of Hyde Park off Grosvenor Square. It was one of the few large hotels in London that escaped bombing. We spent the first weekend walking and taxiing around the city. We were shocked by the damage caused by German bombing, much of it still evident four years after the end of the war. At the hotel guests needed a five shilling voucher to purchase a meal in the hotel restaurant. The shilling was worth about 20 cents. Five shilling meals were pretty bad consisting of lots of mashed potatoes, gravy over boiled brussel sprouts, and a small portion of meat. Hotel guests, however, could order a better meal through room service.

Our floor steward, whom we got to know because he had a brother living in New Jersey where our home was, suggested that we go for dinner at the Cafe Royale in Piccadilly Circus, which had just reopened after being completely destroyed in the Blitz. Our steward made reservations for the same night that Prince Philip, Princess Elizabeth, and Princess Margaret were there celebrating Elizabeth's twenty-third birthday. Esther insisted that we stay after dinner, which gave me concern because there were no prices on the menu, and I did not know if I had enough pounds to pay the bill. She wrote in her diary, "The dinner, after attending an Old Victoria Theatre Company Revival of School for Scandal, included Sir Lawrence Olivier and his wife Vivien Leigh, who played the parts of Sir Peter Teazle and Lady Teazle. Princess Elizabeth wore diamond earrings and an ermine jacket over a blue taffeta silk gown. Princess Margaret wore diamond earrings, an ermine jacket, and a pink taffeta silk gown. The royal party left at 12:30 am." We thought both the sisters very attractive and unassuming.

As soon as possible I visited Jack McDougall and his colleagues at the Chapman & Hall offices, which were adjacent to Methuen's. We had been forewarned by the English publishers, particularly by Sir Stanley, that we probably were going to have some difficulty getting permission from the Board of Trade, the governmental agency that would have to license our subsidiary, but out publishing friends were very anxious for us to make the effort. I visited the London branch of our principal bank, then the Guaranty Trust

Company, and a commercial officer in the American embassy. He made a number of helpful suggestions, asked me to report the outcome of my undertaking, and arranged an appointment for me with the senior officer at the Board of Trade.

At the Board of Trade my first conversation was with a senior officer, probably a career minister, who politely listened to my presentation, asked a number of questions, and said that the person I really ought to see was another officer to whom he referred me. He was the first of perhaps a dozen high level bureaucrats with whom I met; all dressed in the traditional dark jacket and striped pants. The next man to whom I was referred also politely listened to my presentation, asked a number of questions, and said that I really should see still another colleague who was more directly concerned with such matters. This went on from office to office, and I finally realized that something strange was going on. I went back to the hotel for lunch and resumed my campaign in the afternoon, ending with the first man that I had seen. I pointed out to whomever would listen that starting an English company would be a great advantage to England because this would provide employment for people. Finally I found someone who said, "Yes, we will grant you a license provided you print in England every book that you propose to sell in Europe and the United Kingdom." I said, "That is impossible. Some of the books would only sell fifty copies a year. Others would sell in the hundreds, and those, of course, could be manufactured here and a lot cheaper." I pointed out that the books that would sell the most would be modern scientific text and reference books reflecting the wartime research in which American and English scientists played such an important part. I particularly mentioned mathematical statistics and nuclear science. "No," he said, "It has to be all or none." And that was the end of the exercise. As requested I reported my unsuccessful effort to the commercial officer at our embassy.

This unforeseen turn of events made it necessary for us to re-examine our agency agreement with Chapman & Hall. Although we had no interest in extending it beyond the United Kingdom, I did impress upon and Jack McDougall and Alan White, Methuen's managing director, that it would be absolutely necessary, if they wished to continue the relationship, for them to carry a working inventory. I had learned while visiting booksellers with Jimmy Durrant, assistant to the sales director, that Chapman & Hall's practice was to replenish inventory only when a title was exhausted.

Booksellers complained bitterly about this, some even pointing out that they permanently lost business because scientists in particular frequently visited Paris where they could readily buy whatever books they needed. Chapman & Hall agreed to carry out my request solving part of our problem for the time.

Besides Alan White, Jack McDougall introduced me to Methuen's two top publishers, Peter Waite for educational books and John Cullen for trade. That turned out to be a very useful introduction because their arrangement for copublishing in the US was not satisfactory. Methuen had a good list, especially a series called the Methuen Monographs. They were small, inexpensive pocket books in chemistry, physics, and biology written by distinguished scientists, books which could be used by undergraduates as well as graduate students for personal references. Fortunately for us Methuen's copublishing agreement could be terminated with the result that we took over the series, which enjoyed a great success. Subsequently Peter Waite and I went around to visit author prospects at Oxford and Cambridge where we sought additional monographs, text, and reference books with worldwide sales potential. I also used my letters of introduction to visit top scientists at the Manchester Institute of Technology and at the office of the US Navy Scientific Attaché. The real work of this organization was done by a staff headed by Dr Gene E. Sunderlin, who was a Rhodes scholar with a PhD in chemistry. Gene, who would become a friend, and his staff also introduced me to people at various English universities.

After I returned to the US, Chapman & Hall hired an engineer to be the head of their technical publishing program. He came to New York, and I took him up to the Massachusetts Institute of Technology. We were the publisher for the MIT Press at the time. This helped him understand the kind of books he might select with the hope that they would be accepted for copublishing by Wiley.

Generally I found it very frustrating to be working with people in London. The pace of business was very leisurely. I could not make appointments, except with the US naval research people, before ten in the morning. Two hour lunches were standard followed soon after by tea.

From London we crossed to the continent taking the night train to Paris. There in that beautiful city, which was essentially unscathed during the war, we were welcomed by a warm, pleasant spring. The telephone system was such, however, that it was almost impossible to reach anyone except by going to his place of business to make an appointment. As a consequence, we spent a good bit of time walking the streets of the city. In due course, I was able to meet most of the leading scientific and technical publishers and to visit a number of well-located, reasonably well-stocked bookstores.

The most interesting publisher that I met was Mr Freymann, the owner and director of Hermann publishing. He had acquired the rights to publish a British edition of Norbert Weiner's *Cybernetics*, which we had copublished the year before with MIT Press. Freymann was an extraordinary person. Before the war, he had been in the polymer business in Mexico. He sold his business and went to Europe eventually meeting his French wife while working at the Mexican embassy in Paris. His wife's family owned Hermann, but her male relatives had decided that they were not interested in continuing in publishing. So Freymann took over. He continued to live in Paris throughout the war in a lovely apartment overlooking the Luxembourg Gardens. Not surprisingly he aroused the sus-picion of the Gestapo, whose headquarters were in the park across the street from his apartment, and he was regularly called in for questioning. His solution to that problem was simple and obvious. He would always ask his interrogator how many Germans were interned in Mexico, which in fact were several hundred. He, on the other hand, was the only Mexican in Paris. End of discussion.

We became quite friendly with Freymann and his charming wife and found their apartment fascinating. It was a whole floor in a large building with an incredible art collection, which literally covered the walls from the floors to the high ceilings. Some of the paintings were interesting, some were mediocre, others were awful, but most were pretty valuable. In addition, he had accumulated a fine collection of rare books by buying whole libraries when they came up for sale or auction and reselling the unwanted volumes.

Arguing that the US was the largest English-language market in the world, I tried to persuade Freymann to sell us the rights to a number of his books so that we could translate them. "That is not so important" was his usual response. Many of his authors were Communists who had fought in the resistance. One day when we were meeting with an author who was a Communist, Freymann quietly gestured at the author's lapel where he was wearing a peace emblem. The Communists were arguing at that time that the Marshall Plan, which had begun in 1947, was an attempt by the US to take over French culture.

From Paris we went to Zurich on the famous Orient Express, which was back in business with each car marked according to its final destination. In Zurich we visited the Swiss Federal Institute, often referred to as the MIT of Switzerland, and the famous engineering firm of Brown Boveri. At Brown Boveri we were received graciously, but we noted an air of uncertainty on the part of our hosts. Brown Boveri was manufacturing the gas turbine engine, an important new byproduct of the development of the jet plane. Although these engines were undoubtedly covered by all sorts of patents, I thought that maybe the Swiss were hesitant to show me around because they were concerned that I might be an industrial spy of some sort. In general the Swiss were quite secretive and little information of editorial value could be obtained.

From Zurich we took day trips by train to Basel and Geneva to visit some technical publishers and then were booked to return by train through France to the Netherlands. The weather for the most part when we were in Switzerland was pretty bad. So I suggested to Esto that we could fly to Amsterdam in an hour and a half by Swiss Air, an idea which Esto did not take well to since she had never been in an airplane. She wasn't quite sure she wanted to start off in a foreign country. After some discussion, she agreed, and we were able to stay longer spending a very pleasant weekend in Geneva. When we took off in a DC-3 Esto shut her eyes and wouldn't open them again until we were over the Alps.

The weather en route was beautiful. As we crossed into the Netherlands, we could see millions of tulips in bloom due to the early spring. The whole country looked like a huge bed of tulips. We stayed in the Hague, which I used as a headquarters from which to visit booksellers and publishers. Right across the lovely tree-lined square in front of our hotel (the des Indes) was the old and distinguished Nijhoff publishing house, which was headed by Maurits Nijhoff. We had a pleasant conversation during which we learned that we had few publishing interests in common because he was a scholarly publisher. As the conversation drew to a close, I was quite startled when he asked me if I was accompanied by my wife. He explained that he was married to an American and would like the four of us to get together. I left his office, crossed the square, and hardly had time to get to a restaurant when Sylvia Nijhoff, a tall, handsome, middle-aged Texan, burst upon the scene.

Maurits and Sylvia's hospitality turned out to be a gratuitous turn of events because the Nijhoff's were frequent guests at the parties at the US Embassy. They knew the cultural officer, who was a New York publisher on leave, and arranged for us to attend many parties, including a Dutch favourite, a bridge party, which took place at the Nijhoff's. This was our first experience playing bridge in a foreign country, and it certainly was different from what we had experienced at home. People came promptly at the appointed hour, had some refreshment, sat down, and seriously played bridge for two hours, had a closing refreshments and just as promptly departed. Somewhere along the way we were told that it was customary in the Netherlands to tip household servants. I protested that this was an unAmerican practice, and despite pressure from Esto, refused to tip. Somewhat sheepishly I went back the following morning and tipped the Nijhoff's maid.

In Einhoven I visited a number of booksellers and universities as well as Phillips, the huge electronics firm. Phillips published many saleable books written by their scientists in English, and I thought that we might be able to put together a joint imprint a la our arrangement with General Electric. But that never flew. I did all of my traveling alone and by train and was impressed by how the Dutch had so successfully restored their transportation system, which had been stripped of everything, rails, overhead wires, and rolling stock, by the occupying Germans. While I was working, Sylvia showed Esto the sights.

We left the Hague on a local train to Amsterdam where we boarded a through train from the Netherlands across Northern Germany to Copenhagen. Denmark at that time was one of the largest markets for English-language books. Along the tracks we could see vivid evidence of the effectiveness of the Allied bombing and fighter plane attacks on the German transportation system. At every station in the major cities there were heaps of rail cars that would never roll again. Along the way we stopped at Bremen and Hamburg where the locals examined us closely not having seen many American business people since the war. Copenhagen, like Paris, had not been damaged during the war except superficially.

On the *Queen Mary*, we had met a Danish statistician who was writing a book for the statistics series that was being put together by Walter Shewhart, our advisor at Princeton University. As you might expect of a Dane, he assured us that he would make every effort to make our visit pleasant and filled with hospitality. Our author was very helpful introducing me to numerous academics and research scientists.

My most important contact in Copenhagen was the world-renowned atomic physicist Niels Bohr, director of the institute which bears his name. Bohr was a pioneer in explaining the nature of the atom and quantum mechanics. Before the war Bohr had been working on a book on nuclear structure and nuclear fission with John Wheeler, a young physicist from Princeton. They had analysed the fission process, and Bohr had showed conclusively how U 235, not U 238 underwent fission. This discovery led directly to the development of the atomic bomb. In 1940 before Denmark was overrun by Germany, I invited Bohr, at Wheeler's suggestion, to write a much-needed book on atomic physics. We signed a contract, but the occupation of Denmark by the Nazis brought an end to our correspondence. Bohr, who was half Jewish, refused to collaborate with the Nazis and ultimately escaped just before his arrest by crossing the Oresund at night in a small boat.

From Sweden, he was flown to England in the bomb bay of a small plane that carried British dispatches. The pilot had to fly above the range of the Nazi anti-aircraft batteries in Norway. Strapped in the bomb bay, Bohr was provided with oxygen, but did not hear the pilot instruct him to turn on his supply. For a time he was unconscious. The pilot finally realized that he had lost communication with his passenger and flew at a lower altitude, which brought Bohr back to consciousness. From Sweden Bohr went to Los Alamos, New Mexico, where he worked on the development of the atomic bomb under the pseudonym Nicholas Baker. His fellow employees were forbidden to mention his real name. During this time John Wheeler was questioned by the FBI as to whether I had any knowledge of Bohr's whereabouts. Meanwhile my file of correspondence with Bohr disappeared from my office without a trace. I suppose that it was taken by the FBI. In 1958 we finally published a book by Bohr, *Atomic Physics and Human Knowledge*, a collection of seven of his lectures about the lessons that he learned from his study of quantum physics.

In my conversation with Bohr in Copenhagen he told me that he was certain that the scientific discoveries which brought about the atomic bomb and later the nuclear bomb could not be kept secret. He had argued even during the war that the US should immediately inform all countries about the nature of this new weapon and should take all possible steps to head off a nuclear arms race. For years he urged politicians to become statesmen in an effort to bring to an end the production of nuclear weapons.

From Copenhagen, we went to Stockholm where I made the usual round of visits and met with the head of Almquist and Wiksell, Sweden's leading scientific publisher. These conversations led to our copublishing a number of books in English. Our last night train trip was to Oslo where we met several booksellers, and I visited Professor Tom F. W. Barth, a Norwegian who was formerly a tenured professor of geology at the University of Chicago. Barth was working on *Theoretical Petrography*, which we published in 1952. Barth had resigned from his position at Chicago immediately after the war and managed to move his wife and car back to his beloved Norway where he played a major role in restoring the university to its prewar excellence. In the Scandinavian countries, scientists had no difficulty in using the English language books so the market was quite substantial and growing.

To get back to London we planned to fly from Oslo to Glasgow to visit the family of Esto's brother-in-law and then to complete our trip by train. Esto was not exactly pleased, but was comforted when she learned that the SAS planes were flown by American pilots with over-the-water experience. I was surprised when we got to the airport to find that there were such huge crowds standing around doing nothing. It was some kind of national holiday, and for recreation some of the people went out to see the airplanes come and go. Ten weeks from our arrival we departed for the US aboard the *Mauretania*.

When I returned to New York, I made a number of recommendations: first that we set aside temporarily our ambitions to register a company in the United Kingdom until the economy improved and the Board of Trade became less restrictive in its practices. Instead we should aid and abet Chapman & Hall to be more efficient in their distribution operations, which they succeeded in doing, but only to a certain extent, and to put together a more thorough, specific campaign for authors to be published either directly by Wiley or in collaboration with either Chapman & Hall or Methuen. I also recommended that we hire someone to represent us in Europe. Burgess Whiteside took this job moving to Zurich in 1949. Burge had been the managing director of the American Macmillan's British subsidiary; he had organized the company and started it up. Somehow or other he had had a falling out with George Brett, the authoritarian president of the Macmillan Company, and had joined the alumni association of people whom Brett had terminated abruptly. Burge represented us to the bookstores in Europe while Chapman & Hall continued to serve the UK accounts.

Esto and I returned to Europe in 1951. By this time we had developed all kinds of publishing relationships and had more authors in Scandinavia. That was a very useful trip because I got more widely acquainted with the difficulties of the European market. On the first trip I noted that there were problems because of a lack of foreign exchange and because of the lack of convertibility of the various Western European currencies. One could exchange all currencies in Switzerland, and I did find one bank in London that would exchange foreign currencies for dollars. By 1951 foreign exchange had become more readily available to booksellers. The restrictions were slowly but surely disappearing. In general the most noticeable changes had taken place in England. By 1949 very little reconstruction had taken place, and under a Labor government, there were all kinds of strikes and work interruptions. England was far behind France, where there were two economies, the official economy and a very efficient black market economy. Switzerland, of course, was an island in a sense, but even on the first trip to the Netherlands things were in better shape there than they were in England. There was less damage in the Netherlands except for Rotterdam, which was virtually destroyed. The same was true of Scandinavia where the Gestapo had murdered a lot of people in the underground except in Sweden, which was neutral. By 1951 the economy had begun to improve. That was the year of the Festival of Britain. The most important thing that had happened in England was the huge growth in higher education that accompanied the construction of the red brick universities, such as the University of Sussex, which is located less than 40 miles from our offices in Chichester.

After 1951 we made regular trips to England and Europe. In later years we attended the International Book Fair in Frankfurt. The first fair was in 1949. Fred Praeger played a major role in getting the fair underway. He was a Viennese, who became an American intelligence officer in occupied Germany. He became a successful publisher and printer in Vienna and later in New York and then Colorado. Fred had helped provide American assistance to German publishers, such as Springer and Thieme, who were relocating out of the Soviet zone into the west. Fred exhibited our books to the extent that he could get them setting up a couple of planks on boxes.

By the time I started to go to Frankfurt in 1956, the fair grounds had been reequipped with quonset huts with straw mat flooring, and a few of the hotels were back in business. The Frankfurterhof, *the* hotel in those days, was only partially rebuilt; one part of it was still under reconstruction. Not long after the fair opened everyone was hacking, coughing, and sneezing because of the dust that seeped up from the dirt floor through the mats. As I recall the exhibitors were primarily sci-tech publishers including a number of the former East German houses which had relocated to the West including Brock Haus, the encyclopedia publisher. There was also an exhibit put on by the British Council. In contrast to the exorbitant prices charged for everything at more recent Book Fairs, a bottle of wine cost about $1.25. After the fair we visited a number of the German booksellers who had attended the fair. We had taken a lot of photographs, but these proved to be the source of embarrassment because some of the women with the gentlemen in the pictures were not their wives.

After the fair, Burge Whiteside and I went on to Berlin and took a taxi into the eastern sector. This was in the days before the wall was built. The contrast between East and West Berlin was very startling. East Berlin was grey and gloomy. There were practically no automobiles and few people on the street. Everywhere we looked we could see the awful buildings that the Russians had built in a very monumental style. In the West there was still a lot of rubble from the bombing, but there was much more construction. There was no way that the East Berliners could buy books. They had no foreign currency.

We continued to consider ideas about setting up some kind of editorial office in London, but did nothing until the late 1950s when our international business had grown to the point where we simply had to take over our own distribution in Europe. By 1956, for example, international sales had reached $1.3 million, which was 21 per cent of total sales. At the time we were selling $284,000 worth of books in England through our arrangement with Chapman & Hall and saw the potential for much larger sales. In 1957 Martin Matheson and I informed Methuen and Chapman & Hall that the time would probably soon arrive when we would be setting up our own subsidiary in London. We had found that our relationship with Chapman & Hall was hindering our ability to compete in the British textbook market with other American publishers, such as McGraw Hill, Van Nostrand, Addison-Wesley, and Prentice Hall, all of whom either had London offices or were in the process of setting them up. The 45 percent discount that we had to offer to Chapman & Hall and the high conversion rate (8 shillings [40 new pence] to the dollar) that they used in billing us simply made our books too expensive. Moreover, Chapman & Hall had shown little interest in seeking textbook adoptions either by using complimentary copies that we offered them or by visiting professors on campus. We later found out from other American publishers that the distribution of complimentary copies was not an accepted practice in England, a fact that we found most welcome. The British aversion to calling on professors came from the very traditional belief, as Warren Sullivan, the vice president who headed our marketing division, described it, that "the sacrosanct professor should [not] be disturbed in his learned reveries." We also had a number of books suitable for the growing technical college market, but here again Chapman & Hall was not interested in promoting the sales of these books. A number of our authors had visited Chapman & Hall's offices in London and had come away unimpressed saying, as Sully noted at the time, that they doubted "if the physical aspects of their office had changed since the days of Dickens."

I wrote to our British colleagues that we would entertain any proposals that they would like to make that would meet our requirements, but they chose not to respond until the next year. Peter Waite came to New York in the spring of 1958, and again I brought up the matter, but Peter said nothing in response. Then when Sully and I went to Frankfurt for the Book Fair in the fall, we expected to discuss our respective plans with the principals at Methuen and Chapman & Hall given the large concentration of managers there, but again nothing happened. Finally we were tipped off by Halfdan Lynner, who was a Methuen director, that Sully and I would have to bring the issue to a head. We went to London after the Book Fair and asked Alan White for a meeting, which he agreed to after some hesitation.

When we met on October 24, Sully and I laid out our position. It was a matter of prestige for our authors that Wiley have and English company. Also given the exchange rate used by Chapman

& Hall and the 45 per cent discount, our gross margins were unfavorable. Besides our own distribution system, we needed an editorial and production base for adapting American textbooks for the British and European markets. It immediately became clear to us why our British colleagues had been stonewalling. They were afraid that Wiley was going to start an original publishing program that would bring to an end our copublishing arrangements with Methuen and Chapman & Hall. I explained that this was not our intention: it would be wrong for an American publisher to enter the British market as a competitor for original British manuscripts. (We soon changed our minds about this.) Instead we were going to further our cooperation with Methuen and Chapman & Hall. We ended the meeting by telling our British colleagues that we would have a proposal for our future plans ready for our December board meeting and that they should do likewise. After the meeting Sully and I agreed that it would probably take until some time in 1960 to set up a subsidiary. We were encouraged by finding out that the British had recently lifted the restrictions on the establishment of American subsidiaries.

When the time came the Chapman & Hall proposal did not address the issues. We gave them one more chance to make a counterproposal, which they did and which we rejected, and then we began putting together plans for our first foreign subsidiary. It was a modest start. Burge Whiteside was the obvious choice as managing director. So he moved from Zurich to London in 1959 and set up shop temporarily in a two-room suite in offices that we shared with an engineer who was a Chapman & Hall author. The office was located in Pump Court in the Middle Temple in the very center of the old city's barristers' quarters. John Wiley & Sons Ltd was incorporated on November 17, 1959, my forty-seventh birthday.

We got quite a bit of advice and support from Talbot Peterson at Morgan Guaranty, A.C. Unthank of Barton, Mayhew & Co., and Peter Marriage, our solicitor, from the firm of Slaughter & May. Peter became our corporate secretary. Burge and Sully began looking for staff. Of course, we received job applications from people at Chapman & Hall since our part of their distribution business was going to be closed down. Best of all Jim Durrant applied; so did his boss, but we turned *him* down. Jimmy was the bright young man who had been my escort back in 1949. He was forty-one when we hired him and had been working at Chapman & Hall for twenty-two years after surviving the war as an infantryman. He was the right person to run the warehouse since he had been dealing with our books for more than ten years and had pointed out to me long ago the deficiencies in Chapman & Hall's distribution arrangements. He was also a very skilfull marketer, adept at all sorts of promotional activities, and could run the office in Burge's absence. The second person we hired was Ray Hennessey, who had worked in publishing, with scientific bibliographies, and owned his own bookstore. His job was to service our bookstore accounts. For our university representative we hired Mike Colenso, who had just graduated from the University of Witwatersrand and then left South Africa because of his opposition to apartheid. Although he was only 21 and had had only one other job and that briefly, he turned out to be a very effective sales representative. Early in 1960 we rented office and warehouse space at Gordon House on Greencoat Place near Victoria Station. In September, we opened for business.

Twelve years after my first frustrating attempt to license a subsidiary with the Board of Trade, we had finally established our first foreign subsidiary. Within the next decade, we expanded our operations to Mexico, South America, Australia, and Japan. With the opening of our London offices, Wiley was on its way to becoming an international company, but it would take ten more years before we became truly global.

In 1961 we acquired Interscience Publishers. Interscience was a refugee publishing house started in New York by Maurits Decker and Eric Proskauer, both of whom had fled Europe. Interscience's best-known contributions to scientific publishing were the *Journal of Polymer Science*, its successor, the *Journal of Applied Polymer Science*, and the *Encyclopedia of Chemical Technology*, which is now in its fourth edition. The encyclopedia was considered the backbone of their publishing program, which included books in chemistry, earth science, food technology, and library sciences.

The interscience acquisition broadened the range of our publishing programs. It also identified us more clearly as a professional and reference publisher under Proskauer's editorial guidance and enhanced our status as a premier scientific publisher, particularly in Europe. The merger also took us into journal publishing for the first time although it was a number of years before we started publishing significant numbers of journals.

The acquisition gave new impetus to our plans to develop an editorial program in England, plans which we had talked about as early as 1948. Dekker and Proskauer pushed for the establishment of a European publishing company, and we were sympathetic to their ideas. We would spend the next few years trying to start and stabilize a publishing program based in England while figuring out what kind of presence we needed on the Continent.

Interscience had a small sales and editorial office in London run by Fritz Weg, the son of one of Eric's former employers while Paul Rosbaud was working as an editor. Rosbaud was an Austrian, who had edited a metallurgical journal in Berlin before the war. He stayed in Germany during the war to spy for the British. The Germans were working on developing the atomic bomb and needed heavy water, which was shipped from a hydro-electric plant in Norway to Gottingen. Rosbaud reported on these shipments, which then became targets of the Royal Air Force and saboteurs. Rosbaud, who was a very accomplished editor, had worked previously for Robert Maxwell at Pergamon, but had departed as one of the many disenchanted victims of Maxwell's devious practices and arrogant treatment of his staff. Interscience also had another editorial advisor in Europe and was about to hire a third in Vienna to work closely with the Russians.

With the merger we soon outgrew our original quarters on Greencoat Place. We had moved the Wiley offices into the Interscience offices in Chancery Lane while Interscience moved their operation to Greencoat Place. When this didn't work out, we moved the combined operations to Glen House, a new office building in Stag Place near Victoria Station, and retained the Greencoat Place warehouse.

Without consulting with me, Dekker hired Ronald Watson from Butterworth Scientific to build our editorial program. Watson, working with Rosbaud and Ossian Goulding, another Interscience editor, went to work setting up an editorial division, but there were problems. Their first books were from contracts signed with European authors by New York editors that were turned over to London. Many of these were Interscience projects, which Watson described as "massive Teutonic tomes difficult and expensive to produce and almost impossible to sell." These "tomes," by the way, continued to sell quite well in the American market. Watson's own plan was to begin by focusing on journals and books in a limited number of subjects, namely mathematics, physics, chemistry, and earth science. Their second priority list included economics, history, and engineering, but no solicitations for manuscripts were to be made in these areas at first.

In New York we were putting an increasing emphasis on textbooks. Accordingly we urged Watson to do likewise. At first he was resistant. He pointed out that enrollments in England alone were growing fast enough to justify a textbook program for university and technical college levels. But he concluded that it was premature to start a fullscale textbook program because of the need for consolidation in their editorial department, the rapid changes taking place in curricula, the lack of experienced sales representatives, and the cost of textbooks. In 1964 Watson replaced Burge Whiteside, who came to New York to head the international division, as managing director, and the next year he and Ossian Goulding, his chief editor, committed the company to publishing a higher percentage of textbooks. The two of them then decided to divide the editorial department into two divisions, one for textbooks, the other for progressional and reference books. They moved Jamie Cameron in from sales to head the professional and reference operation and hired Michael Coombs to head the textbook division. But they still were publishing only a handful of textbooks. Watson, however, had identified some talented editors, and eventually Mike and Jamie began to make permanent changes in the editorial program.

Watson found a mess in the order processing department when he took over from Burge. They had installed an IBM computer, but only one person had been trained to use it. It was taking up to twelve weeks to process an order, no credit for returns had been issued, and there was no statement of accounts. The effect on their cash flow was catastrophic. Watson reported his findings to New York, and Andy Neilly, who succeeded Sully as vice president of marketing, and Fran Lobdell, our treasurer, went over there to help him straighten things out.

Soon there was another disruption because of our need to move again. The rent on our fancy new offices at Glen House was high, and we were having problems keeping out employees. At that point in history there was close to full employment in London. Jobs were in abundance, and the supply of people could not meet the demand. The result was that on a Monday one never knew who was going to come back to work again since people were paid on Friday. What was happening, for example, was that one of our employees would have a friend who worked some place else in the area. The jobs were pretty standard office jobs, and the perks, which were luncheon vouchers, were standard. The friend would say to our employee,

"Look, why don't you come work with us? We have a much better pub than you have." This became quite a serious problem.

When we moved from Greencoat Place to Glen House, Burge put together a long-range plan that called for moving all but our editorial offices out of London. So I appointed two search committees, one made up of people opposed to relocating out of London and one made up of people who thought we should get out. We were also influenced by the fact that McGraw-Hill had relocated out to Maidenhead northwest of London, but had not managed to get away from the disadvantages of competing in the London job market.

Fairly soon after the study groups got underway, they agreed that we had to relocate. At that time we had what was called a forward warehouse down in Chichester operated by Gibbings Harrison, a former tannery business. Chichester was close to Southampton, the port of entry for our books. Shipments would come in—we were carrying ample stocks in those days—and we wouldn't have room for them in our London warehouse. We would take what was needed immediately, and the rest of it would be on call in Chichester. From there we could replenish our supply as needed. Eddie Harrison told Watson about an interesting office building in Chichester on Baffins Lane. It had been a Corn Exchange as recently as the postwar years. When we looked at the building, it was only a shell and was still showing the signs of its past. There were lots of pigeon droppings and feathers, and the old derrick for lifting bags of corn up to the second floor was still in place.

We decided that the Corn Exchange would do. We signed a lease at one quarter of the London price with no increase for fourteen years. Then we decided, unwisely as it turned out, that the local warehouse company which had been running our forward warehouse would be capable of running our new combined warehouse as a contractor. When this arrangement became increasingly unsatisfactory, we looked for a new location for our own warehouse. In due course we arrived at Bognor Regis, a town just outside Chichester where there was the equivalent of a new industrial park. We were the first people to take a lease there and put up a building.

We moved our operations to Chichester in May, 1967, which meant replacing 80 per cent of our employees. Only fourteen people remained with us from the London office. Esto and I were there for the official opening of the office on June 1.

Naturally enough all of this caused a certain amount of disruption.

Despite this sales were running ahead of budget. Still we could not figure out exactly what was happening with the British editorial program and particularly with textbook publishing. In late 1967 we sent Charlie Stoll, head of the college division, to Chichester with a list of questions that we needed answering. There were a number of problems, according to Mike Coombs, who was, in effect, the textbook publishing program at the time. One was the size of the European textbook market. Even though it was growing, it was not large enough to support the origination and development costs of new textbooks. Chichester needed additional sales in the US market to justify these costs, but Mike's books "fell between the marketing interests of the New York college division and the scientific and engineering reference division." Additionally, European academics were less accustomed to adopting and writing textbooks than their American counterparts.

The problem of a European textbook publishing program was partially solved when we began publishing Wiley International Editions (WIEs) in 1965 in a partnership with Toppan, the Japanese printing and publishing company. These were inexpensive, paperback editions of our major textbooks. Chichester imported them from New York and sold them in Europe and subsequently began publishing a few International Editions of their own.

In 1970 Eric Proskauer was given additional international responsibilities. Mike Colenso and Eric focused on the problem of making our English company more of a European company, something that we had been concerned about since my first trips to Europe. Mike wrote a strategy paper that argued that Europe was essentially a collection of language markets rather than national markets with English the largest market followed by German, French, Spanish, and Italian. For the English language market, he noted that Chichester was successfully and profitably selling Wiley International Editions, but that in some years there were not enough new titles. In his paper he asked if Chichester should build up its textbook program to fill the gaps in the supply of WIEs, but concluded that English language textbooks really needed to be published on the basis of the large American market. With German there was a different situation. Mike argued that advanced level scientific books should be published in English, but there was a major opening for a German language program at the lower level. He noted that Eric had spoken of the need in Germany for "a Proskauer in reverse"—that is, a German editorial person who would either be found in Germany or sent there as an editorial director.

Watson was resistant to setting up a separate editorial operation on the continent. There was also concern in Chichester that we were going to break the company into two parts by setting up a separate distribution facility on the Continent. Again this was an idea that we had been discussing since my earliest trips to Europe. This idea combined with Eric's emphasis on becoming a European publisher rather than a primarily British publisher was very threatening to Chichester.

Responding to Mike's paper, Eric proposed that we begin a phased move toward setting up a German publishing company focusing on textbooks in computer science, management, and psychology. He thought we should use the sale of translation rights and copublishing arrangements with German publishers to solicit more information on the German market. This would also help us get leads on German publishers who might be available for acquisition or a joint venture. In 1971 we set up John Wiley & Sons GmbH in Frankfurt to publish German translations, but I don't recall that anything much came of this. At the same time Charlie Stoll was exploring the possibility of having Ossian Goulding set up an editorial office in Zurich, but again nothing happened. Ultimately the decision was made to reduce the emphasis on textbooks and focus more on the high margin publications that were more typical of Interscience publishing.

Watson finally retired in 1976. He had had a difficult time establishing an editorial program, and the support systems necessary for its success. Fortunately he employed people, like Jamie Cameron and a young genius named Peter Ferris, who did understand and successfully solved many of these problems.

In fairness to Ron, part of his problem could have been his increasing deafness since his hearing had been badly damaged during the war when he was in the army.

In 1976 we sent Marianne Orlando, our international vice president, to Chichester on a regular visit. Marianne reported that Watson was in splendid health. He must have had a stiff upper lip; within a matter of days, he was in the hospital for an ear operation, and he never came back to work again, suffering through repeated operations in his retirement.

Having set up an English subsidiary, we continued to be concerned as Dekker and Proskauer had been about what kind of publishing and distribution presence we needed on the Continent. The dialogue between New York and Chichester went on for years, but never very conclusively. Essentially we were trying to work out the correct relationship between our New York publishing programs and the publishing program of an autonomous subsidiary. The problem was how to coordinate our respective publishing and distribution operations while allowing a subsidiary to retain its independence. As we grew as an international publisher, our New York international division grew accordingly. It eventually became an unwieldy bureaucracy. When we began to reorganize and refocus all of Wiley's operations in the late 1980s, Charles Ellis recommended that we eliminate the international division. In its place we emphasized closer coordination and consultation between editors and publishers in both college and professional, reference, and trade publishing in Chichester and New York. Our managers in Chichester, particularly Jamie Cameron, Mike Foyle, and now John Jarvis, also developed a strategy for becoming a European publishing company. We set up editorial offices in Paris and Strasbourg and then acquired Verlag Chemie in 1996. We had reached a new phase in the internationalization of Wiley. Our English subsidiary was finally becoming a European company.

CHAPTER ONE

The Move

HOW WE DID IT

Michael Colenso (former Marketing Director)

THE MOVE from London to Chichester was in fact the third move after Wiley Ltd had been established in the UK. From the original premises in London's Inner Temple, a skeleton staff of five had planned and set up the company. The Inner Temple is the area of London between Fleet Street and the Thames which is occupied by barristers' chambers, and the quiet courtyards are peopled by bewigged and begowned scions of the legal profession on their way to and from court ruminating pleasurably on their usurious fees.

Behind the elegant Georgian exterior of number 6 Pump Court lay our cramped offices with plywood partitions which precluded

Wiley in London

Ron Watson, Managing Director

Marjorie Redwood, Managing Editor

Harry Newman, Assistant General Manager

Jim Durrant, UK Trade Manager

confidentiality. The plumbing arrangements were, it seemed, genuinely Georgian, and the heating system produced environmental conditions which varied between stifling equatorial and bracing arctic.

If producing your first invoice is the true sign of being an operating business, then this momentous event occurred in September 1960 at Gordon House, Greencoat Place, London SW1. Gordon House was a former warehouse of the Army and Navy Stores. The building lay a block or two behind Victoria Street and, on the third floor, accommodated the 1,500 or so titles which Wiley then had in print, plus an office staff of nine people; there were also two representatives on the road.

The acquisition of Interscience and the launching of a British publishing programme meant that new premises were needed and the company took a staggering 7,000 square feet of office space at the mind-blowing price of £2.10 per square foot in Glen House, Stag Place, also just behind Victoria Street. This spanking new building housed most of the office staff, by now about forty in number, in conditions of unaccustomed modernity and great style. The reception area provided a complete library of Wiley and Interscience books and sported formica-topped occasional tables under ganglia of cylindrical downlighters; chairs were militantly functional in a style then called "Swedish", from Hille and Co. The whole fitting out seemed quite profligately expensive at the time. Order Processing and the books remained warehoused at Gordon House in considerably less splendour.

In the palmy days of the 1960s, with higher education burgeoning throughout Europe, English the undisputed language of science, and research flourishing, the business problem was how to accommodate the growth that Wiley, in common with all scientific publishers, was effortlessly achieving.

In London salaries and the cost of office space were escalating alarmingly, staff turnover was rising in an overheated London economy, and the Government sought to engineer an exodus from the capital. An organisation called the Location of Offices Bureau, (LOB), subsequently more trendily renamed London Outward Bound, was established to provide help in moving businesses out of London to relieve the pressure on the capital. The done thing was to head for the provinces to improve the quality of employees' lives, reduce regional unemployment and occupy cheap premises.

Among the first tasks confronting Ron Watson after he took

Mike Foyle, Europe Trade Manager
(became Managing Director in 1983)

Mike Colenso, Sales Manager (Marketing)

Ossian Goulding, Editor

W Bradford Wiley, Chairman, and
President of John Wiley & Sons Inc.

over as Managing Director from Burge Whiteside, was to find a long-term home for Wiley Ltd. We had outgrown the Gordon House warehouse, for there were now 2,200 titles in print and an unprecedented 250 new books per year. Following an advertisement in the *Bookseller* Gibbings Harrison, a former tannery in Chichester, had won a contract to handle overflow warehousing.

Research into relocation patterns for businesses quite clearly shows that after conducting exhaustive analyses of long-term space needs, employment patterns, local infrastructure, communications, etc., the most important determinant in the choice of the new location is the personal preference of the Managing Director. Ron Watson was a keen golfer and if St Andrews was plainly impossible, Goodwood provided a tolerable alternative.

Proximity to Gibbings Harrison certainly influenced the decision, as did the excellent hospitality of Eddy Harrison, the company's principal. Regular train services from London were soon to be upgraded: it took 1 hour 40 minutes from Chichester to London,

---

BRITISH JOURNAL OF APPLIED PHYSICS   VOL. 11, SEPTEMBER

John Wiley & Sons Ltd
a subsidiary of the New York scientific and technical publishing house of John Wiley & Sons Inc., opened its London headquarters on 29th August, 1960.

John Wiley & Sons Ltd
aim to ensure that any reader may speedily obtain through his bookseller any of the 1,200 current books, and to keep him informed of its forthcoming titles.

John Wiley & Sons Ltd
will maintain and further existing editorial liaisons with British publishers and authors towards joint publication for the fullest benefit of world markets.

John Wiley & Sons Ltd
are grateful to Chapman & Hall Ltd. for the fellowship that has attended the 65 years of their now terminated agency of Wiley books in the United Kingdom, and their sincere and continuing co-operation.

John Wiley & Sons Ltd
would be pleased to enter your name on their mailing list at its new offices in Gordon House, Greencoat Place, London, S.W.1, (Telephone VICtoria 0143).

The announcements which appeared in the national press in 1960/61

John Wiley and Interscience Merge

John Wiley & Son, Inc., and Interscience Publishers, Inc., have merged the two companies to establish one of the world's largest publishing houses devoted entirely to the production of books and journals in the various fields of natural and behavioral sciences, technology and engineering. The London subsidiaries of the two companies will also be integrated into a single marketing function servicing customers, authors and booksellers throughout the U.K. and Europe.

Operating under the name of John Wiley & Sons the combined enterprise will offer an integrated line of scientific publications, including textbooks, encyclopaedias, research monographs, scientific journals, abstracts and paperbacks. The Interscience publishing programme will continue as a distinct Wiley division.

W. Bradford Wiley has been elected President and Chief Executive Officer of the new company, and Edward P. Hamilton will serve as Chairman of the Board. Maurits Dekker and Eric S. Proskauer, respectively President and Chairman of the Board of Interscience, will become Vice-Presidents of Wiley and members of its Board. J. S. Snyder will become Vice-President and Secretary, and Francis Lobdell has been appointed Vice-President and Treasurer. Other members of the Board include J. S. Barnes, Jr., and Andrew H. Neilly, Jr., both Vice-Presidents. Mr. J. B. Whiteside will be Managing Director of John Wiley & Sons Ltd., the London subsidiary.

John Wiley & Sons Inc., is one of America's oldest publishing companies, having been established in 1807 in a small bookshop in the Wall Street district. Interscience Publishers was founded by Drs. Dekker and Proskauer in 1940.

Wiley has in excess of 1,500 titles in print, and we publish about 150 new books in any of 106 subjects every year. It makes you wonder how many you missed when you think there are many major companies with the same sort of record.

In order that you will not miss any Wiley titles we produce a Preview every two months which lists the books we expect to publish, and summarises those that we have published during the preceding six months.

Starting soon, we hope to produce an advance information card (so dear to the hearts of most librarians) on every new book we intend publishing and then of course there are the promotional sheets which we put out on many of our books.

Lastly, have you got our catalogue—257 pages long with 66 pages of indexing where you can lay your finger on any Wiley title with remarkable ease.

If you are not getting the necessary promotional material for your library, please drop us a line, we are anxious to keep you informed.

JOHN **WILEY** & SONS LTD.

Gordon House,
Greencoat Place, London, S.W.1

then; now, thirty years later, it takes a mere 1 hour and 40 minutes! Above all the Corn Exchange was available on a long lease at a price per square foot which was less than half of that we were paying in London.

Viewing the Corn Exchange for the first time revealed why this singular economy was possible. The building was derelict except for a substantial population of pigeons demonstrating their habitual incontinence, and a number of warfarin-immune rodents of spectacular size. There was no heating and the roof was in a terminal state of dilapidation. Some original corn traders' desks of potential antique value remained, but they were magically spirited off, I suspect by the local architect Stanley Roth and his enthusiastic partners.

Chief among these partners was Geoffrey Claridge who, having masterfully disguised his disbelief that an international publishing house of high repute was actually considering taking a lease on the premises, emanated reassuring confidence and mobilised great energy in rendering the building habitable. C. W. Pile, a local Chichester builder, undertook the conversion and Geoffrey and I jointly designed the interior layout. Geoffrey was consistently supportive, as is demonstrated by a remark I well recall after I had

An early exhibition (Space Age chairs for an expanding publisher)

Staff in the London office

chosen green slate to front the reception desk; this, he assured me, would give the library the general ambience of a Wimpy bar.

London staff were invited to spend weekends in the area at the company's expense to look for places to live. Mondays, back at Glen House, would see ugly scenes in the corridors as it was discovered that colleagues had put in competing bids for the same house. Worse tensions occurred when employee A described to employee B the uninhabitably awful place they had viewed over the weekend, only to discover that employee B was negotiating to buy it.

Chichester staff were recruited locally and shipped up to London to work alongside those whose jobs they would soon be doing. Surviving this tested their mettle to the extreme. In the end all but one senior manager and the greater proportion of the middle management decided to move. Those who had chosen redundancy had to be induced to stay to the last moment because the job market was so bullish in London. The new Chichester staff proved excellent. In short, despite misgivings and the traumas of change, the move was a positive and amicable event.

We moved over the Spring Bank Holiday (still Whit in those days) in May of 1967 in a military-style operation, with every item of furniture, nay, every pencil sharpener, colour coded and labelled to assure its delivery to its precise final destination. I remember it

Mike Colenso (former Managing Director), Bart van Tongeren (non-executive director), Joan Colenso; (photograph taken at Stationers' Hall in 1982 on Wiley's 175th anniversary)

as a warm and oppressive day, and I also remember being thoroughly exhausted by the end of it. Staff, new and old, had the rest of the weekend to sort out their work areas, and on the Tuesday morning, after the long Whit weekend, the company started up again without missing a beat.

We had retained a service office in London because most of us were sceptical about the willingness of overseas visitors to undertake the visit to Chichester. In the longer term the London office proved unnecessary and Wiley added to its eminence as an international publisher the versatility of being a good local citizen in the city of Chichester and in the county of West Sussex.

RECOLLECTIONS OF AN ASSISTANT GENERAL MANAGER

Harry Newman (former Assistant General Manager)

It was May 1962 when I joined Wiley as a (not so young) newly qualified chartered accountant. At that time the company was to be found in Greencoat Place, Victoria, London, on the third floor. The number of staff, including the warehouse personnel, was around 25. There were two other small offices, one in Chancery

Lane and the other in Fleet Street. These two offices were occupied by the recently recruited editorial and promotion departments.

The company, which was first registered in August 1960 and commenced trading in 1961, was formed to take on the task of marketing and selling the products of the parent company, tasks preciously carried out by Chapman & Hall (now part of the Thompson Group). There were no editorial, production, journals or data processing departments in those days. The Managing Director was an American gentleman, Burge Whiteside, Tommy Traill was the Financial Director, and Mike Colenso and Jimmy Durrant were Marketing and Sales. Ron Watson had just been brought in to set up the Editorial department with Marjorie Redwood as his assistant and Ossian Goulding as editor, later to become Editorial Director.

The company, which in its first year had supplied only the UK market, was now given the task of taking over supplying the European market; previously this had been dealt with direct from the USA. The invoices in those early days were prepared by using an Adrema machine, which produced the invoices by means of a plate which stamped out the names and addresses of customers and the titles of the books. The sales and bought ledgers were prepared on National Cash Register accounting machines with a separate card for each purchaser and supplier. The nominal ledger was written up by hand.

The parent company had in 1961 merged with Interscience Publishers, whose products were mainly professional and reference-type books and journals (Wiley having been in the main a college textbook publisher). In my first year I had the task of preparing the final accounts for Interscience as well as the Wiley accounts, dealing with two firms of auditors. In those days the accounting year was 31st December.

Salaries and wages were paid in cash fortnightly (every two weeks for our American colleagues), with one or two exceptions. One week a call was received from the Warehouse complaining that the wages had not been received. Investigations into the whereabouts of the messenger resulted in his being found at a local hostelry calmly sipping a pint of the local brew, with the wages bag tucked safely under his seat.

In October 1962 the company moved into new offices on the third floor of Glen House, Stag Place, Victoria, leaving the Warehouse staff in the old building. The process of employing staff for the Editorial and Production departments was then begun. Early members of this team were Jamie Cameron and Mike Coombs. The first books published in the UK were Prigogine's *Advances in Chemical Physics* Vol. 5 and Lundqvist's *Forensic Science* Vol. 2.

Responsibility for the Customer Service, Accounts and Personnel functions lay with the Financial Director, as did all service functions. The company's pension scheme (which was and still is a non-contributory scheme) was set up in 1962; at this time it was a fully insured scheme run by Scottish Widows, with J.H. Minet acting as brokers. It has since become a managed fund scheme.

The first venture into data processing was the purchase of an IBM 444 tabulating machine which produced the invoices and sales ledger accounts. The task of transferring from the National Cash Register system to the new IBM system was not without its problems. The Adrema machines were dispensed with and we moved into the punched card era, where cards were produced for each title, in either single or multiple units, with separate cards for the names and addresses of customers. With a large order it was not unknown, for staff to select the various titles and then drop the whole pack on the floor. Long fingernails did not last long in this department.

In 1967 the company, which was rapidly expanding, required more space. Offices in the Victoria area were expensive, and so it was decided to move outside London. The task of finding a suitable site was given to Ron Watson, Tommy Traill and Mike Colenso, who each visited different sites. In the end it was decided to relocate the offices to Chichester and to place the warehousing and distribution with an outside agency (Gibbings Harrison of Chichester) on a ten-year contract. Staff were recruited locally in Chichester and a number were brought to the London office to receive training prior to taking up their appointments in Chichester. One such person was Marion Fisher, who is still with the company. The present Baffins Lane building, which was at that time a derelict grain store, was refurbished and then leased from Taylor Woodrow. (We could have purchased the freehold for a fraction of today's rent, but our masters in New York preferred to put their money in books rather than real estate.)

In 1977 the contract with Gibbings Harrison was cancelled and the distribution centre in Bognor was built. All stocks were moved from our agents. The move had many problems and it was some considerable time before we were straight again. Round-the-clock working was the order of the day, and staff from all departments were encouraged or coerced into helping with the resulting backlog of orders; even the Managing Director (Adrian Higham) was pressed into service; although after a short while it was decided that his talents lay elsewhere. One thing I learned from this experience was never, never to build up a backlog of returns.

THE PROMOTION CHALLENGES

Alan (ASH) Hawes (Promotions)

Before being able to decide how to approach a different, and hopefully more effective, way to promote Wiley's titles, I had the problem of trying to understand what each book was about. I was having trouble understanding the authors' names, let alone the titles or contents! (OK, hands up those of you familiar with *Friedel Crafts and Related Reactions* by George Olah—I don't even know what Olah means.) What a relief to discover that Wiley's bestseller at that time was an unusually understandable title, *Basic Organic Chemistry*, by an even more understandable pair of names—Cotton and Wilkinson. (Sir Geoffrey Wilkinson died earlier this year, aged 75.) Indeed, this book was so successful it was rumoured that competitors McGraw Hill and Academic Press were considering putting out a *fatwa* on Jim Durrant.

So, there was the set-up; delightfully quaint and relaxed, but not selling too many books. Since I had originally been briefed to bring professionalism and fresh thoughts from the garish sphere of advertising to the rather intellectual and rarefied world of publishing, it seemed to me time to use the well-established techniques of selling: concentrating on the presentation and ignoring the plot. Eventually, with an ever-increasing team, the panoply of sales promotion was gradually brought into effect.

That today's highly sophisticated ways of selling a staggering number of books has evolved over the last twenty years is hard to imagine, but congratulations to everyone concerned: you've really "got a result".

TO BE PUBLISHED ON 11TH NOVEMBER...

VOLUME I
ENCYCLOPEDIA OF POLYMER SCIENCE AND TECHNOLOGY

PLASTICS—RESINS—RUBBERS—FIBRES

Editorial Board: HERMAN F. MARK, Chairman
NORMAN G. GAYLORD, Executive Editor
NORBERT BIKALES, Associate Editor

The first truly comprehensive source of information on the science and technology of polymers (including resins), rubbers, plastics, and fibres. The complete work will comprise some 10 to 12 volumes of articles by international authorities; the articles will cover all phases of the preparation, properties, processing, and uses of polymers. Each volume will have about 960 pages, 7½" × 10¼", fully illustrated and cloth bound. The general format is uniform with the well known:

Kirk-Othmer ENCYCLOPEDIA OF CHEMICAL TECHNOLOGY

Subscription price per volume for the whole set £15.0.0. Single volume price £18.15.0.

An assessment of the depth of coverage may be made from the following list of articles which will appear under the letter 'A':

ABLATIVE POLYMERS
ABRASION RESISTANCE
ABRASIVES
ACETYLENE AND ACETYLENIC POLYMERS
ACIDS, MALEIC AND FUMARIC
ACIDS AND DERIVATIVES, ALIPHATIC
ACIDS AND DERIVATIVES, AROMATIC
ACROLEIN POLYMERS
ACRYLAMIDE POLYMERS
ACRYLIC ACID POLYMERS
ACRYLIC ELASTOMERS
ACRYLIC ESTER POLYMERS
ACRYLIC FIBERS
ACRYLONITRILE POLYMERS
ADDITION POLYMERIZATION
ADHESION AND BONDING
EFFECT OF CHEMICAL CONSTITUTION
THEORY OF ADHESIVE JOINTS
ADHESIVE COMPOSITIONS
BONDING
APPLICATIONS
EVALUATION
ADSORPTION
AEROSPACE APPLICATIONS
ALBUMINS AND GLOBULINS
ALCOHOLS, MONO AND POLYHYDRIC
ALDEHYDE POLYMERS
ALFIN CATALYSTS
ALKALI METALS AND DERIVATIVES
ALKALINE EARTH METALS AND DERIVATIVES
ALKYD RESINS
ALKYLENIMINE POLYMERS
ALLENE POLYMERS
ALLYL POLYMERS
ALUMINIUM COMPOUNDS
AMINES
AMINO ACIDS
AMINO RESINS
ANIONIC POLYMERIZATION
ANNEALING
ANTIBODIES AND ANTIGENS
ANTIFOAMING AGENTS
ANTIOXIDANTS
ANTIOZONANTS
ANTISTATIC AGENTS
AQUEOUS POLYMERIZATION
A-STAGE
AUTOMOTIVE APPLICATIONS
AZO CATALYST

A fully descriptive prospectus is available

JOHN WILEY & SONS LTD
Glen House, Stag Place
London, S.W.1

WILEY

science editions

Designed both for general readers and students, SCIENCE EDITIONS paperbacks encompass every major area in the world of modern science.

Architecture, Astronomy, Biological Sciences, Computers, Earth Sciences, Education, Economics and Business Administration, History Mathematics, Philosophy, Physics, Political Science, Psychology, Sociology—these are the subjects in which over 60 volumes have been published and 20 more are scheduled to be published early in 1965

Inspect and purchase them at
HEFFERS PAPERBACK SHOP LTD.

WILEY Interscience

Introduction to Advanced Field Theory

G. BARTON, *The Clarendon Laboratory*

This book is Volume 22 in the series *Interscience Tracts on Physics and Astronomy*, edited by R. E. Marshak. Based on lectures given at the Clarendon Laboratory, it emphasizes the field theory of elementary particles, and orients the reader towards what can and cannot be done without reference to the iterative solution. The author assumes the reader is acquainted with the outlines of covariant perturbation theory and with Feynman diagrams. In elementary terms, he explains why the problems treated and others like them are of interest in physics, and presents enough basic detail and discussion so that the reader can assimilate current papers in this field, with a reasonably clear understanding of their relevance to the theory as a whole.

176 pages, 49s.

Symposium on Optical Masers

edited by JEROME FOX, *The Polytechnic Institute of Brooklyn*

Volume 13 in the series *Microwave Research Institute Symposia* The symposium, held in New York City, April 16-18, 1963, depicts the rapidly advancing optical maser field in mid-stride, presenting a balanced display of its electrodynamical, statistical, material, and practical features. It attempts a comprehensive integration of the physics and technology bearing directly on the discovery, theory, and application of maser phenomena at optical and infrared frequencies.

677 pages, 113s.

Plasma Waves

J. F. DENISSE, *Observatoire de Paris* and J. L. DELCROIX, *Faculté des Sciences de Paris* translated by M. MEINRICH and D. J. B. DANIEL, *General Electric Research Laboratory*

Number 17 in the series *Interscience Tracts on Physics and Astronomy*, edited by R. E. Marshak, University of Rochester. Containing a systematic and concise description of waves in plasma, it treats the theory of small amplitude plane waves in an infinite plasma.

160 pages, 59s.

**Glen House
Stag Place, London, S.W.1**

INTERSCIENCE *announce*

POLYMER PREVIEWS

A new monthly journal, the first issue, May 1965

POLYMER PREVIEWS will preprint the synopses of the papers to be published in the *Journal of Polymer Science*, Parts A (General Papers) and C (Symposia). These synopses will be published 4 to 6 weeks after acceptance of the original articles. For easy reference to the complete paper, they are identified by title and author and by a code number carried into the final publication.

POLYMER PREVIEWS is published:

To provide a rapid survey of the important new contributions to research in the field.

To provide advance information on the essential contents of all papers to be published 4 to 6 months later in the *Journal of Polymer Science*.

POLYMER PREVIEWS will start publication in May 1965. To ensure prompt receipt place your subscription now with your agent or with

JOHN WILEY & SONS LTD. GLEN HOUSE, STAG PLACE LONDON, S.W.1

Annual subscription, including postage, $11.00 (79s.)

Congratulations to
HUDSON BOOKSHOPS LTD.
on opening yet another branch

•

Hudsons of course are well known for their comprehensive range of quality books, so naturally their Technical and Scientific sections are just crammed with Wiley and Interscience titles.

John Wiley & Sons Ltd. · Glen House · Stag Place · London SW1

...ry of Wood
L. BROWNING, *The Institute of Paper Chemistry*, Wisconsin

The purpose of this book is to present the outstanding features of the chemistry of wood and its components. It is written for the scientist, technologist and student of wood chemistry, who wants critical if not exhaustive surveys of the topics included.

690 pages. 189s

Administration of the Chemical Enterprise
edited by CONRAD BERENSON, *Assistant Professor of Business Administration*, Bernard M. Baruch School of Business and Public Administration, the City College of the City University of New York

Provides an overall picture of the commercial aspects of the chemical industry by drawing upon the experiences of a large number of the firms in the field. A basic exposition is given of such vitally important topics as marketing, management, advertising and promotion, personnel, patent law, accounting and finance, all written with a specific emphasis upon the chemical process industry's special problems and practices.

448 pages. 87s

Models for Production and Operations Management
E. C. BUFFA, *Professor of Production and Operation Management*, University of California

The objective is to present an introduction to the analytical methods that have been developed for people in operations research management science, and industrial engineering and to undergraduate students. The book is written in relatively non-mathematical style and his attempted to present contemporary concepts and ideas without indulging in over-simplification.

644 pages. 70s

John Wiley · Interscience
Glen House · Stag Place · London SW1

JOHN WILEY INTERSCIENCE

WILEY Interscience

Publishers of books in Science Engineering and the Social Sciences

Our 1964 Complete Catalogue of 546 pages includes books on

AERONAUTICS
CHEMICAL ENGINEERING
COMPUTER ENGINEERING
APPLICATIONS & PROGRAMMING
ELECTRICAL ENGINEERING
ELECTRONIC DEVICES
CIRCUITS & SYSTEMS
FOOD SCIENCE & TECHNOLOGY
GLASS MANUFACTURE
MANAGEMENT SCIENCE
OCEANOGRAPHY
PETROLEUM & MINING ENGINEERING
PHARMACEUTICAL CHEMISTRY
PHOTOGRAPHY
PULP & PAPER
ETC.

Are you on our SUBJECT MAILING LISTS?
An application form will be sent on request

JOHN WILEY & SONS LTD
Glen House, Stag Place
London, S.W.1

IF YOU HAVE WRITTEN, or better still intend to write, we invite you to get in touch with us. We publish in all fields of science and our representatives would be glad to meet you anywhere in Europe to discuss your plans.

Your book would be speedily produced and published in London, either under the Wiley or the Interscience imprint. Our sales organisation is world wide and you would also benefit by simultaneous publication in London and New York.

JOHN WILEY & SONS LTD.
GLEN HOUSE, STAG PLACE,
LONDON, S.W.1.

AL AGE
30 March 1963

ENTIRELY REVISED AND REWRITTEN

Announcing publication on May 8th of Volume 1

KIRK-OTHMER

ENCYCLOPEDIA OF CHEMICAL TECHNOLOGY

SECOND EDITION

Volume 1.
Approx. 960 pp. 7¼" × 10¼". Illus. Cloth.
Subscription price 260s. Single volume price 338s.

Executive Editor:
ANTHONY STANDEN,
Interscience Publishers, a division of John Wiley & Sons, Inc.

To be complete in 18 volumes of about 960 pages each. A guaranteed subscription price of 260s. per volume for the whole set is available for a limited period.

John Wiley · Interscience
Glen House · Stag Place · London SW1

BUSINESS AND INDUSTRY

Prize book was published by local company

The Lanchester Prize, an international award made by the Operations Research Society of America, has been given to a British author, Stafford Beer, for his book "Decision and Control," issued by British publishers John Wiley and Sons Ltd., of Baffins Lane, Chichester.

The book was considered by an international committee of experts to be the best book on operations research published anywhere in the world in 1966, and won its place against formidable world competition from many established experts on the subject.

The award brings great credit to the author and publisher for an outstanding achievement in a field of knowledge in which, so far, American authors have been pre-eminent since the original development of the concept of operations research in the United States.

The author now has had more than 20 years of practical experience in active leadership of this, his chosen subject, has been known as a philosopher, scientist and manager. One of the European leaders in the interdisciplinary science of control and cybernetics, he has pioneered its management applications.

He is a member of many scientific, educational and Government organizations and committees, author of more than 100 publications, and well known as a frequent lecturer and broadcaster.

BUSINESS AND INDUSTRY

Publishers' new catalogue is a massive affair

The Chichester publishing company of John Wiley and Sons Ltd. has now issued its new catalogue containing more than 3,000 titles of medical, scientific and technical works published by the company and its international associates.

The catalogue, the first the company has published since it moved to Chichester last June, has for its front cover an aerial view of the city taken from a photograph of 1947 in which the focal point is the present location of Wiley's offices in Baffin's Lane.

The photograph is reproduced by Wiley's with acknowledgements to the book "Georgian City" written by Dr. Thomas Sharp and published by Chichester City Council.

The list of titles in a Wiley catalogue is for the most part strictly for the more esoteric of initiates, but there is also a fair sprinkling of others more accessible to the average intelligence and more appealing to it.

One of these in the new catalogue is "Perception of People and Events," by two lecturers in psychology, Peter B. Warr, of Sheffield University, and Chris Knapper, of the University of Saskatchewan, who is also a graduate of Sheffield.

The book is attractively presented in a thoroughly readable fashion, and is illustrated with expressive and descriptive cartoons. Its aim is not only to communicate with those who are already familiar with the issues raised, but also to interest others so that they will move on to become experts themselves.

from Chichester Observer

JOHN WILEY—THIRTY YEARS AGO: AN ACCOUNTANT LOOKS BACK

Ronnie Gorlin (Accounts)

When John Jarvis asked me for a contribution to a book celebrating Wiley's thirtieth anniversary of their arrival in Chichester I was amazed. "Why me?" I asked. "Because you were there at the time," came the reply. Slowly it dawned on me that John was right. I had come down to Chichester as a young manager on the consulting side of Arthur Andersen, who are still the company's auditors. Wiley were about to install their first computer system and Ron Watson, the then Managing Director, thought some help was needed.

Chichester and indeed the John Wiley offices have changed very little in thirty years. The city is somewhat more crowded, the offices much bigger and more hi-tech, but superficially at least they still strongly resemble their younger and smaller selves.

Ron Watson, a tall, courteous publisher, was still finding the shock of moving to Chichester somewhat traumatic. He explained it to me this way. "The office closes at 5 p.m. It takes me ten minutes to cycle home. A large gin and tonic is a necessary restorative after a busy day—but living so close I can get plastered by 7 p.m." For the first time I realised that living close to the office might not be an unalloyed advantage.

I was made very welcome by Harry Newman, the Financial Controller. Many current staff will remember Harry's gentle and kindly manner and his great unflappability. However, he explained he understood nothing about computers—which I subsequently learned was quite true—and that he had a bright young man of twenty who was going to be a real boffin, called Peter Ferris. When Peter and I were introduced it was difficult to tell who was the more surprised and disappointed, but each attempted to conceal his feelings about the other, which can be succinctly summarised as "Gosh—I bet he knows nothing about computers". It is true that in the world of the blind, the one-eyed man is king; and unfortunately it was Peter who had the eye. My attempt to get even by drafting in a bright young man from Arthur Andersen called Bob Dymond was reasonably successful, and between Peter and Bob the first IBM 360/20 card computer was successfully installed.

At this time Mike Colenso was Marketing Director. He was very

Ronnie Gorlin

able and ambitious and he expressed his views trenchantly. He was always a man in a hurry. As with many computer system installations, crises had to be overcome and deadlines met, and this meant that one weekend just before the system went live I had to be in Chichester. Mike Colenso generously asked my wife and me to stay and we retain the happy memory of superb meals (Mike's wife was a wonderful cook) and a lot of drink. On the Sunday afternoon I went to the office and, in the computer room, Bob Dymond and Peter Ferris were arguing about the correct approach to solving a last-minute hitch. As I came in they stopped and looked at me, and said almost in unison, "It's your responsibility. You decide." It was obvious I was incapable of deciding on the basis of the technical argument. I looked at them both and decided to back Peter. After all, he was the one who wanted to make a career at Wiley. Fortunately my decision was correct and Peter has been a respected director of the company for some years.

Soon after the move to Chichester there was a major financial and accounting problem for Wiley which was also important for the country: the sterling devaluation of 1967 and the substantial reduction of sterling sales and assets, when expressed in dollars. Although not involved in the audit at the time, I was still involved with some of the meetings that ensued, including the first discussions on dollar billing because of the risk to sterling. The £/$ exchange rate movements became an important topic of discussion from that time onwards. It was in the aftermath of the devaluation that I first met visitors from the parent company, including Brad Wiley himself, who always had a soft spot for the UK business. Brad was of course a highly capable businessman, but he was much more. He was enormously good company. Even though I was much younger, he was always easy to talk to. I learned a great deal about the publishing world from him. His Chief Executive was Andy Neilly, whom I also met on various occasions. He was not particularly interested in the parts of the business where I was most involved, and our most animated conversations were about the American Civil War, on which he was a great expert.

My final memory of the Wiley of thirty years ago is very much from the Arthur Andersen angle. It was always a very popular assignment to be on the Wiley audit—the people were friendly, the business was interesting and there were usually some interesting accounting points. I can no longer speak with the same authority about the accounting and audit points, but certainly the friendliness of the people has remained and the interest of the publishing business and all its challenges has increased.

MUSIC AND MINGLING ON THE MIDDLE FLOOR

Marion Fisher (thirty years at Wiley)

On 27th May 1967 the big move from Stag Place, London took place. About 50 staff worked through the Bank Holiday Monday, ready to open for trading on Tuesday 28th May 1967—this was so as not to upset the customers and to continue with their orders. It took us about a couple of months to get straight, but as far as I know not a single file or desk went missing. The celebrated opening party was one to remember with all the New York dignitary here.

After that came the Christmas parties with food and drink on the top floor and music and mingling on the middle floor, but of course we were only talking about 50 to 55 staff in those days. Everyone knew each other, we were people to management and they all had time to stop and have a word. Even at Frankfurt time the Wileys came over, and Mr Bradford Wiley along with Charlie

Stoll always came to each department and gave us a talk, a bit like the quarterly talks we used to have. The biggest get-together was the pound devaluation—all new price sheets had to be printed and sent out. What an operation! All hands to the pump, not like the automatic photocopy machine we have today. No, it was a machine called a duplicator with a big ink drum and stencil. While two people ran these off, the rest of the staff including Mike Colenso (who was the sales manager), his wife Joan and Mike Foyle's wife Margaret both heavy with child, came in to help send these price lists out as quick as possible. Then when we had finished we had another party. In those days life was one long round of parties—any excuse. We even had to put our midwives' hats on one day—the girl who worked in the computer room went into labour.

In my days as a cashier and wages clerk as I was known then (none of the fancy titles of today—we were all known as clerks or secretaries) I had to take over the wages from six different wages people: those in London, then three in Chichester, from May 1967 to April 1968 (end of the tax year). What a mess and an awful lot of mistakes to sort out, but I got there. Our banking in those days was only about £900 to £1,500 a day, and over the years it grew. Harry

June 1967—the official opening of the Chichester office, attended by Brad and Esto Wiley and many booksellers and publishers. With the Mayor, Alderman R. Stephens, are (left to right) Ron Watson, Esto Wiley, Mrs Watson, Mrs Stephens, and Brad Wiley

Newman bought me and my colleague a cream cake for our first million. The accounts payable was paid by manual cheques, all typed by me, around 70 to 100 each week. The wages were paid weekly in cash. I used to go the bank with one our postroom men in those days and walk back with about £1,500 to £2,000 in cash in our pockets. The monthly ones were paid every other week, all done by cheque and sent to their banks by me.

We moved along for a few years then we acquired the Distribution Centre in Bognor for our customer service and warehouse in 1977. That is when we started to grow, but Harry Newman always made a point of visiting Bognor once a week, sometimes twice.

There have been a few characters come and go, like the bookkeeper, God rest his soul, always with a self-rolled cigarette in his mouth, ash all down his jumper. Not sure how he would react to our non-smoking office of today, he was a law unto himself. There was also a dear lady who was Mike Foyle's secretary who used to send him off to the hairdresser for a hair cut if she thought it was too long, and bought him cakes as she thought he was far too thin. She was also partial to a sip of gin which she kept in her drawer. Then of course the dear dear Wegs. Mr and Mrs Weg escaped from

The Chichester Team—Jim Durrant, Mike Foyle, Ron Watson, Alan Hawes, Mike Colenso and Andrew Neilly

Brad Wiley with Mr Richard Blackwell on his right. Mr E. Harrison of Gibbings Harrison (Wiley's packers and shippers) is on the left and next to him is Mr Stanley Roth (architect for the modernisation of the new Wiley offices).

the German Occupation with very minimum belongings and set up a publishing business which they called Interscience. Mr Weg who was 70 plus took a shine to one of our tea ladies (we had tea and coffee brought round to our desks) and everytime he saw this tea lady he would shuffle after her as fast as he could. It was like running the gauntlet for the poor tea lady.

As we started to grow, so my work grew. I was assigned an assistant, who introduced the first computerised payroll using an outside computer service. Before this it was all done by hand, with hand-written payslips. All went fine for a few years, then in February 1983 the outside firm went bankrupt overnight. Imagine my horror—near the end of the tax year and no wages. Anyway they kept their side of the bargain and saw us through to the end of March 1983. During February and March my colleague and I started to look for another computer service, and believe me, we saw some horrors. Then thanks to a contact at National Westminster Bank, dear Centrefile set us up for our first payrun for April, and all this time not a soul in the company knew apart from certain management. We still ran two payrolls, one weekly and one monthly. The fortnightly one phased out, then the weekly payroll

Mr Robert Sadler, previous owner of the Corn Exchange Building, with Brad Wiley

phased out around 1986/87, when we persuaded the weekly staff to go monthly. Here we are today with 390 plus staff on the payroll. How things have changed, but far too much to put to paper.

SADLER'S TO MOVE AFTER SELLING CORN EXCHANGE

For nearly a century the farmers of West Sussex congregated at the old Corn Exchange in Baffins Lane, Chichester. But now an era has come to an end.

Modern communications embracing telephones, cars, and travelling salesmen have reduced the need for a corn exchange. It is no longer the only place where a farmer can meet a corn merchant.

Earlier this year, Sadler's (Chichester) Ltd, sold the Corn Exchange, which they have owned for the last 14 years, for a price which has been quoted as "well in excess of £40,000."

Leased to publishers
It has been bought by a holding company and leased to a firm of book publishers. The business in the Corn Exchange ceased about a month ago, and has now moved to a much smaller premises at the market.

In the old days the Corn Exchange fronted on to East Street. Now only the rear half of the building is used as such. The front hall is now the Granada Cinema.

Sadler's who have been in existence for 75 years, transferred their office premises from over their shop in South Street to the Corn Exchange building; but now they are moving farther afield to the Industrial Estate.

Mr Robert Sadler is a trifle sad that his company have severed their connections with the Corn Exchange, but they are moving to a set of modern offices at Terminus Mill, which is being built alongside Sadler's existing property there.

Crawled through

"I can remember my grandfather telling me about when they changed the front of the building into a cinema," he said. "The pillars outside the cinema were lying in the road waiting to be erected, and as they were hollow he crawled right through them."

The company are to move as soon as the new offices are completed, and Mr. Sadler said that it should be in about a month's time. The move will be a great advantage from the aspect of the convenience of building the office alongside the mill.

Inside the extensive buildings there are vast machines for the preparation of Sadler's products to the different specifications put before them.

The company also have a laboratory for scientifically testing their seeds so that they can be guaranteed. This is at present at the Corn Exchange, but will be moved to the new building at the same time.

Chichester Observer, Friday, 30th September 1966

The internationally known London based publishing company John Wiley and Sons Ltd, subsidiary of John Wiley and Sons Incorporated of New York are now known to have acquired Sadlers Corn Exchange as the main Head Office of their Company in Great Britain.

In a recent interview a spokesman for the company, Mr T. Traill, said their association with the City of Chichester started some years ago when Messrs Gibbings Harrison of The Tannery, Chichester, operated an overflow warehouse for them and undertook the despatch of books. His company had been considering for a long time the removal of their Head Office into the country. There was no real necessity for them to be in London, also there was the attraction of lower operating overheads and much more pleasant working conditions for the staff away from the wear and tear of big-city life. After looking into various places all over Great Britain they decided Chichester was in fact the best place for them.

When the company eventually moves only the executives will come to work at the new Head Office, and approximately 70 employees will be required locally.

We asked a local Estate Agent who has been associated with the John Wiley Ltd transactions, for his views on the recent big moves to Chichester by London companies; some attractions seem to be less problems with staffing, housing is much easier and more convenient to the place of work, in addition the rates and rents of premises are lower, rented office space is only a quarter of central London.

Chichester Promoter,
October 1966

ON THE OCCASION OF WILEY LTD'S 25TH ANNIVERSARY

A personal memoir by Ronald A. Watson (Managing Director 1962–1976)

Wiley was founded in 1807 by Charles Wiley who opened a bookshop in downtown New York. He kept no records of the early activity, and his son, John, who succeeded him followed his practice. When Martin Matheson, Senior Vice President in the early 1950s was asked to compile a history of the first 150 years, he had

Ron Watson greeting Mr and Mrs Geoffrey Claridge

THE OBSERVER, FRID

Situations and Appointments

INTERNATIONAL PUBLISHING

FEMALE ADVERTISING ASSISTANT

Splendid opportunity for a young girl, probably between 18 and 22 years, to join a young and interesting team responsible for the promotion of scientific and technical books.

She must be lively, intelligent, imaginative and industrious with typing and duplicating ability and business experience.

Holidays honoured (up to 2 weeks)

Write or phone Susan Bruce-Woodcock

JOHN WILEY & SONS LTD.
BAFFINS LANE, CHICHESTER,
SUSSEX. Telephone Chichester 84531

AUDIO TYPIST
required
For CHICHESTER COMPANY

Pleasant working conditions, 5 day week, holiday arrangements honoured.
Commencing salary, £13 per week at 22.

Box No. S3137
Observer House, Chichester.

SCHOOL LEAVERS AND YOUNG LADIES
are you looking for an interesting career?

We offer you training on the following systems:—
GE115 MAGNETIC TAPE FILE COMPUTER
IBM 029 80 COLUMN CARD PUNCH
IBM 059 80 COLUMN CARD VERIFIER
P203 MINIPUTER
AUDIT 1513/71 ACCOUNTING MACHINE
and a well paid, satisfying job in Chichester's Computer Bureau.

We would like to interview you if you have
(a) Maths "O" level and three other subjects.
(b) keenness and determination to be a successful operator.

Please phone Chichester 84569 for an interview.

P.S. ACCOUNTING SERVICES LIMITED.

PART-TIME WORK FOR LADIES

Work of a light nature in modern glasshouses morning and/or afternoons for the summer only.
Transport available
For details telephone
The Manager,
CHICHESTER 84822

Framptons
NURSERIES LTD.
Chrysanthemum Cuttings Department,
LEYTHORNE NURSERY . CHICHESTER . SUSSEX

TRAINEE ASSISTANT
is required at

THE MIDHURST BOOKSHOP

Applicants should be under 25, and have attained a reasonable standard of education.

Please telephone
Mrs. Rawlins, Midhurst 3168

REDMOOR MOULDINGS AND JOINERY WORKS
BIRDHAM, Chichester

SENIOR WOOD MACHINISTS —
Staff Position

WOOD MACHINISTS AND JOINERS
Required immediately.
Rates of Pay according to experience. Permanent positions.
Ring for appointment: Birdham 381/2 or write to:
REDMOOR MOULDINGS, REDMOOR ESTATE, BIRDHAM, CHICHESTER.

MOTOR MECHANICS
You can't do better than work with the Hares Group

T. H. RUSSELL LTD. — MIDHURST
Telephone 2443

An Experienced Motor Mechanic
required by old established and expanding Company.
Good wages and Sickness Benefits.
For appointment please telephone
Mr. C. W. Cubberley, General Manager

Some advertisements from The Chichester Observer in 1969 illustrate how life was then ...

for Eight Skilled Men

OUR WAGE RATES ARE NEVER KNOWINGLY TOPPED BY OTHER GARAGES IN THE AREA.

Come and talk about it at
THE HARE GROUP HEAD OFFICE
Hares Surrey Street, Littlehampton (7291)

Make an appointment to see how this advertisement can benefit you!

---

of Chichester 86551

A Member of the Army & Navy Stores Group of Westminster.

A Vacancy has occurred for a trainee N.C.R. 32 Operator for the sales ledger section.
AN ASSISTANT COOK IS REQUIRED FOR MORANTS RESTAURANT KITCHEN
Apply Personnel Manager, Morants, Chichester.

R. F. L. SMITH MOTORS
Tangmere Corner, Chichester

STAFF WANTED
FORECOURT ATTENDANT
MOTOR MECHANIC
PAINT SPRAYER or IMPROVER

Telephone Hainaker 258

YOUNG LADY
REQUIRED FOR OFFICE DUTIES
Typing essential.
Apply
W. JONES & SONS
Lennox Street,
Bognor Regis 4641

J. BAKER & CO.
require
SALESMAN/SALESWOMAN
for Men's and Boys' Wear
Apply MANAGER,
66/66a, EAST STREET, CHICHESTER.

OAKHURST NURSING HOME
CARRON LANE, MIDHURST
PHONE 2863

STAFF REQUIRED
DOMESTIC HELP
NURSING ORDERLIES
COOK
PART-TIME GARDENER

TRANSPORT ARRANGED

HALL & CO. (South Coast) LTD
Member of the Ready Mix Group of Companies
BUILDERS' MERCHANTS, RMC HOUSE, LYON ST. WEST, BOGNOR REGIS

have the following staff vacancies:

YOUNG MAN ASSISTANT
FOR TRADE/RETAIL COUNTER.
Experience preferred or training would be given to suitable applicant

GENERAL CLERK
To assist in Pricing Department.
Young man 16-18 years of age, or school leaver.
Excellent opportunities for advancement
Holiday dates honoured

IF YOU
Live in Bognor Regis
Like Driving
Have a Knowledge of First Aid
the vacancy for

AMBULANCE DRIVER-ATTENDANT

can provide a worthwhile career of service to the public.

Basic wage £15 8s. 7½d. a week (less 13s. 4d. a week without a current first aid certificate), plus standby allowances. Uniform provided. Apply to County Medical Officer of Health, Metropolitan House, Northgate, Chichester for further information. Closing date 30th June

---

27,000 HOMES . . . .
how's that for a market? The Observer Classifieds are seen in 27,000 homes each week. If you are buying or selling use the Classifieds for real results.

The Observer Motor Mart

WADHAMS

| 5/6 SOUTHGATE, CHICHESTER | Tel. 82282 |
| BIRDHAM ROAD, CHICHESTER | Tel. 86485 |

Used vehicles in stock on the 14th June, 1969, date shown is the year in which car was first registered unless otherwise stated

1968 (G Regd.) MORRIS 1100 Mark II 2-Door De Luxe Saloon. Green £635

1965 Model (First Registered December, 1964) AUSTIN 1800 De Luxe Saloon. Grey. Wing mirrors £495

1965 M.G. MIDGET. Red. With heater, tonneau cover, fog lamp and wing mirrors £450

1966 Model (First Registered November, 1965) HILLMAN SUPER MINX Saloon. Blue. Wing mirrors £495

1968 (G Regd.) MORRIS 1300 Mark II 4-Door Super De Luxe Saloon. Sandy Beige £715

1967 (F Regd.) M.G. "B" SPORTS. British Racing green with overdrive and radio £895

1966 HILLMAN SUPER MINX Estate. Grey £560

MORRIS OXFORD SALOONS and M.G. "C" SPORTS available for immediate delivery in most colours

WADHAMS BUY GOOD USED CARS AND PAY A TRULY REALISTIC VALUE IN CASH

WADHAM $ STRINGER

little on which to write. This practice of destroying early records continued until this present day, and I, in attempting to record the early history of Wiley Ltd was faced with the same difficulty which faced Martin Matheson.

Let us note in celebrating the first 25 years of Wiley Ltd that it was not the first presence of Wiley in Britain. First there must have been co-publication since we see the imprint on a journal title page "John Wiley, Nassau St., New York and James Paul, Paternoster Row, London, 1834", and ten years later in 1844 "New York and London, Wiley and Putnam." G.P. Putnam, once a clerk employed by Wiley in New York, eventually became a partner. One suspects that his paramount interest was establishing an international copyright law; an interest shared by John Wiley and maintained by the house of Wiley to this present day.

Putnam thought that he could promote the sales of American books in Europe and British books in America if a company were founded in London. This was agreed in 1840 and a shop was opened in Paternoster Row, now sadly bombed out of existence in the last war, but still remembered by the writer of this memoir and many other geriatrics as the cradle of their trade.

From Paternoster Row, Wiley and Putnam moved to Waterloo Square. It seems that Putnam put more effort into international copyright than he did into publishing since the business failed in 1847 and the Wiley–Putnam partnership dissolved a year later.

With the dissolution of the Wiley–Putnam partnership Charles Wiley left the field of belles-lettres publishing and concentrated on science and technology under the imprint of John Wiley & Sons. At first he published in biology, an extraordinary decision in view of the fact that America was expanding westwards in building roads and railways; there was a burgeoning manufacturing industry in the New England states, and American universities were establishing their present pre-eminence. It appears that the trend was reversed by William H. Wiley, an engineer whose work was carried on by Edward P. Hamilton, the first member of Wiley to visit the present writer in London. I believe it was really because he loved to dine with my wife and myself in Rules restaurant, and we were glad to entertain an American gentleman. The Wiley reputation was founded on engineering and technology, and it still persists. The next visitor was Brad Wiley in 1949, looking for the Butterworth Scientific sales agency in America.

At that time I was general manager of Butterworth Scientific and

Medical. Marjorie Redwood and I had founded Butterworth Scientific. She joined me as secretary, but soon became assistant sales manager in charge of internal sales, order processing and the subscription records of our six journals, truly an all-round sales assistant. We also had two editors, one part-time, and a promotion manager. The organization worked on the principle of Occam's razor "It is vain to do with many what can equally be done with few."

I was unable to help Brad Wiley since we were committed to Academic Press and Interscience for our American sales and to Lange, Maxwell and Springer for European sales. I really believe that Brad's excursion into Europe at that time was unsuccessful since all of us were already committed.

Wiley's sole sales agent in Britain and Europe at this time was Chapman & Hall and had been so since 1895. Chapman & Hall were several publishers, but the impact of Wiley scientific and technical books on their sales later caused them to enter this field.

In 1959 Wiley decided to end the association with Chapman & Hall and to re-establish their own company in Britain. The first managing director was Burge Whiteside, an out-going and attractive character of engaging personality. According to Wiley tradition, he had been for some years a college traveller. I heard of the intention to found a company in Britain for sales and promotion of Wiley books when I first visited them in New York in 1959.

The parting with Chapman & Hall was amicable and Burge Whiteside was fortunate in recruiting Jim Durrant as his first member of the new company. I had known Jim for some years. He had worked for Chapman & Hall since leaving school and I believe his wife, Joan, had also. He started work by pulling Wiley books in the warehouse and had gradually became the liaison agent between Wiley and Chapman & Hall.

Burge and Jim visited me at Butterworth a few times and we talked of the problems and difficulties of starting up. Eventually, in 1961 they opened their working office in the Middle Temple. In the midst of lawyers they must have found a congenial niche since Barabbas is reputed to have been the first publisher.

With much hard work, Jim and Burge established relationships with the book trade and eventually were able to found a sales and promotion operation in Greencoat Place in Victoria, in premises which actually were a warehouse. Stock was imported from New

York, staff engaged and the operation was inaugurated with a memorable party on the premises. Many booksellers and publishers attended and it was universally agreed that Wiley had opened shop with considerable éclat.

1961 also saw another important even in the history of Wiley, Inc. Wiley acquired Interscience, the founders Eric Proskauer and Maurits Dekker had left Europe, being Jewish, and had originally come to New York to found a subsidiary of Elsevier. The German invasion of Holland prevented this and together they founded Interscience. Dekker had experience of bookselling in the booksellers Dekker and Nordeman, and Proskauer, a chemist by training, had worked in Leipzig with the Weg company. The Wegs were famous throughout Europe as specialists in geological books. They complimented each other well, Dekker on the sales side and Proskauer, primarily an academic, on the editorial side.

I had known Eric Proskauer for some years. Actually I had worked on his book on polymer science, co-authored with Arnold Weissberger, when employed at OUP. Interscience had a small sales organization in Chancery Lane, London, run by Fritz Weg, son of Proskauer's former employers, and his wife. I had often been invited to Proskauer to join Interscience to establish an editorial presence in Europe and maintain contact with their European authors. Since the second diaspora there were many German Jewish authors and publishers in Europe and America. But Interscience could offer no more than I already had and I told Eric Proskauer that if Interscience ever merged with a larger publishers, then I would join.

At the Frankfurt book fair in 1961 Proskauer told me of the merger with Wiley and asked me to join as editorial director. I joined Wiley in January 1962, Marjorie Redwood coming with me. Fritz Weg moved the Interscience sales operation from Chancery Lane to the Wiley premises in Greencoat Place and we occupied the old Chancery Lane premises. Wiley Ltd had now become a complete publishing operation.

It soon became apparent that the Greencoat Place premises were too small and Burge Whiteside and Jim Durrant looked around for new premises to have us all together. We moved all together into Stag Place, Victoria, retaining Greencoat Place as warehouse and promotion departments. The new office in Stag Place was a "prestige" location, and at £8 a square foot ruinously expensive at that time.

We now had an expanding organization. Mike Colenso joined as a representative in Britain, Mike Foyle and Ove Steentoft in Europe, and Mike Coombs and Jamie Cameron also representing us in Britain. On the editorial side, we had inherited Ossian Goulding and Paul Rosbaud from Interscience and had set up a subediting and production team.

At Butterworth, Marjorie Redwood and I put our major efforts into the publication of journals and "first in the field" books. Thus we were first in molecular chemistry, publishing Synkin and Dyatkina *Structure of Molecules*, first in animal social biology with Hediger *Wild Animals in Captivity*, and first in the digital computer field with Booth *Automatic Digital Calculations*. Our six journals, were all "research" publications.

The editors we inherited from Interscience included an Irishman of note, Ossian Goulding. He was a first-rate contact man and a most valuable member of the team. He could charm the birds out of the trees, and I believe he sometimes did. The other was Paul Resbane, an Austrian who once edited a metallurgical journal in Berlin. He stayed in Germany during the war and was an undercover agent for Britain. At that time Germany was ahead of Britain developing the atomic bomb. They relied on heavy water as a moderator whereas the Allies used carbon. The heavy water was supplied by the hydroelectric plants in occupied Norway and had to be moved by rail from Norway to Guttingen in Germany. Rosebaud reported all movement and little escaped the RAF and the saboteurs. Journalism and international publishing was at that time, and probably still is, a cover for agents worldwide. What has not been told, and cannot yet be fully reported, is the work of another member of Wiley. It was he who ensured the supply of ball bearings from unoccupied Europe, a supply which kept the Spitfires and Hurricanes flying. An old man digresses, but hopefully it adds interest to the story.

Wiley Ltd progressed along the line of every infant publisher, making Wiley Ltd known throughout Europe. The editorial side was strengthened by the translation of Jamie Cameron from the sales side, as was the Wiley tradition but unusual in British publishing. He was followed by Mike Coombs. On the sales side the company was tremendously strengthened by the advent of Mike Colenso, soon to become sales manager whilst Tom Traill and Harry Newman organized the accounting, order processing and warehouse activities. At that time Ove Steentoft, a Danish representative well known to European booksellers took over part of Mike Foyle's burden in Europe.

In 1964 Burge Whiteside was invited to return to New York and assume responsibility for the international subsidiaries in London, Canada, India and Australia, a job [later] held by Adrian Higham. He accepted.

Meanwhile, it was decided that Wiley Ltd should assume responsibility for the production and manufacture of books contracted by Interscience from European authors. These were massive Teutonic tomes difficult and expensive to produce and almost impossible to sell. They consisted for instance of esoteric mathematical works edited by one Radok in Vienna, out-dated series of old-fashioned books on geology such as the series edited by Gansser in Holland and Kalervo Rankoma in Finland, and expensive books on chemistry such as the Patai series. The result was an imbalance on the editorial and production side which prevented us from adhering to our original plan. It was done with the best of intentions, in giving Wiley Ltd a ready-made list of authors and contracts, but they were P&R books which even then were already on their way out.

On the departure of Burge Whiteside to New York, I was invited to become Managing Director of Wiley Ltd. Having been fully occupied in attempting to build a list and at the same time inundated with Interscience manuscripts and author liaison, I knew little of the administration of the sales and promotion side, in Wiley at least.

I had been in the chair for two days and was in process of handing over the administrative side of the editorial programme to Marjorie Redwood. This was no great difficulty as she was competent and responsible for much of it already, besides having experience of all sides. It was a surprise to receive a request from Tom Traill and Mike Colenso for a conference. They asked if I knew the state of the company on the administrative side. I did not, but promised to look into it at once.

The inquest dismayed me. I knew that it was intended to reconstruct order processing and accounting by introducing an IBM 444. A punched-card machine rather like a Hollerith. I also knew that Peter Ferris had been trained to use the machine and assume that training had been given to order processing, returns for credit and the warehouse. Nothing of the latter had been done, and the machine was installed. Soon it was taking us twelve weeks to process an order and no statements of account had been sent out for a similar period. The bookseller would not have paid an account in any case, since returns had piled up and no credit notes issued for several months. The effect on our cash flow was catastrophic, and morale was low.

I told Tom Traill and Mike Colenso that I now knew that position. They advised that I inform New York without delay. I then wrote a letter to our parent company and asked both Traill and Colenso to read it, amend it and agree it. Both agreed that it was a fair statement of the position. As a result, Andy Neilly, their Vice President in charge of sales and Fran Lobdell, the Vice President Treasurer, in charge of order processing, warehouse and accounting in New York, came to London. I went on leave and left them to their inquiry. Burge Whiteside resigned from Wiley Inc. and Marianne Orlando was appointed administrator of the international companies.

The trouble in Wiley Ltd was purely lack of training and arrangement before the IBM 444 was installed. The machine was treated simply as a superior version of the former equipment. Actually it was a primitive fore-runner of our present systems. It was thought to be the servant of the staff, unlike the present situation which borders on the reverse. Staff planning and rearrangement should have been geared to the machine, not the other way about. In the event, nothing was done.

We had no cash flow, relations with our customers had reached an all-time low; it was a case of "all hands to the pump". All hands responded nobly. People from all departments were drafted into order processing and we worked all day and often far into the night making invoices and credit notes, sometimes by hand with ballpoint pens. Eventually order was restored, but with the advent of WI titles our warehouse could not accommodate the stock. Tom Traill replied to an advertisement in the *Bookseller* from Gibbings Harrison, tanners in Chichester for many years. They had specialized in making leather for the soles of Army boots in two wars, but failed probably finding it impossible to adapt to the needs of modern footwear. The tannery business failed and they decided to become warehousemen. Gibbings Harrison housed and pulled WI titles and a few slow sellers for two or three years.

Eventually it became apparent that Wiley Ltd must expand. We could not afford London rents and rates and accordingly decided to leave London. It was thought that I had taken leave of my senses and actually given lunch by the American fraternity of American publishers to try to dissuade me from my folly. Within two or three years almost all had followed by example, including McGraw Hill, our chief competitor.

Meanwhile, Gibbings Harrison in Chichester was handling even more of our stock. Eddie Harrison, who played cricket for Sussex and was an international squash player for England, told us that the old Corn Exchange in Chichester was for sale and Taylor & Woodrow the civil engineers and contractors would purchase it. The interior of the building was a wreck, but structurally the Corn Exchange was sound. Chichester was a pleasant location; it was far enough from London so that people did not commute and it was near Southampton, the port of entry for our stock. We signed an advantageous contract at one-quarter of the London rent with no rent raise for 14 years, and decided to move in May 1967. Messrs Roth reconstructed the building, their plan winning a Southern Counties architectural award.

Less than 10% of our London staff moved with us, but thankfully they were key personnel. To engage local staff we ran advertisements in the local press and soon had sufficient applicants. This was expected in the Chichester of those days. "Publishing is such a gentlemanly profession" but how little did they know of our cut-throat trade!

As the first American company to move into Chichester it was necessary to engender goodwill by not rocking the boat in offering London wages. Accordingly we discovered the local going rates and advertised accordingly. Engaging a room at the Ship Hotel, Tom Traill and I interviewed applicants. We filled our vacancies easily. The applicants were all good quality, but of course, new to publishing. We therefore hired key personnel a month or more before we moved. They commuted to London daily at our expense and worked alongside our experienced staff. We thus required a cadre of semi-experienced staff and were ready to move.

The reconstruction of the Corn Exchange was complete. We had moved our stock into the Gibbings Harrison warehouse a month or so before we planned to move and were ready to go. I had had experience of movement during the war as a logistics staff officer, so the plan was not difficult. In conjunction with Tom Traill and Mike Colenso we planned to move over the Spring Bank Holiday in 1967. Tom was in charge at the London end, Mike in Chichester. We invited the new Chichester staff to help over the holiday, but

A book display at a 1968 management conference

did not require them to do so. Most turned up in working clothes and pushed and shoved all into its pre-planned position. Helped by refreshment both solid and liquid, the move ended in an impromptu party. We moved from London on Saturday 28th May 1967 and opened for business on Tuesday 1st June, four days later. The official opening was attended by Brad and Esto Wiley together with the mayor and mayoress and other civic dignitaries, along with many booksellers and publishers.

Having moved into the provinces, it was necessary to maintain a presence in London publishing. Accordingly, I became more involved in the Publishers Association as chairman of the scientific committee and was able to steer Jamie Cameron on to the journals committee. We also joined the International Publishers Scientific and Medical Association. This was inaugurated in a meeting in Amsterdam, an event which my wife and I have never forgotten.

All worked smoothly in Chichester, having gradually overcome the IBM 444 debacle. We formed a yacht club with our own cruiser. The club is now unfortunately defunct, but the cricket club flourishes, and now there is a Wiley stoolball league. We also became sponsors of the Festival Theatre with the Wiley name on several seats in this internationally known prestigious playhouse.

There were no more alarms and excursions until the devaluation of sterling in 1969. Luckily Ossian Goulding gave us 48 hours warning from Switzerland which enabled us to make financial plans.

The warning was repeated 12 hours later by Ove Steentoft from Copenhagen and confirmed by myself with a call to friends in Frankfurt. We immediately put our plans into operation transferring sterling balances to New York and stopping all invoicing ahead of devaluation. After devaluation was announced I was inundated with telephone calls from American subsidiaries in London suggesting an immediate conference with a view to joint action. I could only say that Wiley had already acted.

Wiley Ltd was growing. We had got rid of most of the Interscience inheritance, had acquired some agencies and above all had started to fulfill our original intention to concentrate on journals. Ossian Goulding acquired *Numerical Methods*, Jamie Cameron had initiated *Software* and others were in the pipeline.

We had to have more space. I therefore approached the Booth family hoping to acquire the Booth Rooms, but they were drawing an income from the premises and would not sell. We then heard that the Granada Cinema might be for sale. Tom Traill approached our landlords, Taylor Woodrow, and they were willing to buy. Granada seemed willing to negotiate, and Messrs Roth, in the person of Geoffrey Claridge, drew plans. The intention was that Wiley should have the top floor, the "pit" was to be a lecture hall, whilst the foyer was to be a hall of boutiques. Then Granada changed their minds and the plan was abandoned. We did not give up, and Harry Newman and I went to see a suite of offices opposite the city museum. It was a warm afternoon and the smell of chickens cooking in the Shippams factory wafting in on the south-west breeze was enough. We left, eventually joining the Shipwrecked Mariners Association in North Pallant.

Shipwrecked we were, for at this time there seemed to be some financial stringency in New York. Marianne Orlando informed us that we were not to increase staff and that wage increases were to be held at a minimum. This was a blow as it had become apparent that Gibbings Harrison could not cope with our expansion and we were looking for our own warehouse. The years in Chichester had seen one rational financial crisis after another. It was necessary to plan for each one as it occurred. This new stringency came just as the British financial horizon seemed a little brighter.

As it happened, I became ill and after six months in hospital I was obliged to resign. Ten years, and nine surgical operations later and a further six months in hospital have caused me to lose touch with Wiley. Once I knew every one of our 115 staff, now I only recognize two or three, though I often see and talk with our original members in Chichester.

Note: Ron Watson died in June 1995

CHAPTER TWO

Wiley in the 1970s

A NEW MANAGING DIRECTOR

Adrian Higham (former Managing Director)

"WELL, what do you want to do now?" The question came as a bit of a shock. It was my first day at Wiley, 17th May 1976, and I had been there about an hour. Marianne Orlando, Vice President, from New York, had come over to introduce me. We met for breakfast at The Dolphin & Anchor and presented ourselves at Baffins Lane at 9 a.m. to be met by the three directors, Harry Newman (Finance), Mike Foyle (Marketing) and Jamie Cameron (Editorial). I remember that one or two of the senior managers were wheeled in and there was a somewhat desultory discussion of the company structure, and then the question was put. I was on my own! My mind was a blank. I suggested we might walk round and shake hands with the staff, and that is what we did—all eighty or ninety of them. So started my six very enjoyable years as Managing Director of Wiley Ltd.

As part of my introduction I held a series of days away from the office with each department, to understand the details of the business and meet the individuals concerned. The preparation for each of these days proved to be a learning experience, and not only for me. I found I was demanding information not asked for before; and whatever was asked for, the Computer department run by a young enthusiast, Peter Ferris, promptly provided. It was a new and refreshing experience. It was during the day spent with the Editorial department that it became clear that the whole profitability of the company, with its turnover of about £3 million, depended on two journals, *Numerical Methods in Engineering* and *Software Practice and Engineering*. We had only six Wiley Ltd journals at the time and Jamie Cameron was keen to expand the programme, and that is just what we did.

The establishment of our own warehouse at Shripney dates from this period. We created our own invoicing system and then waited with bated breath when we first went live. It took an unconscionably long time for the first books to come off the packing line. It was an uncomfortable period. We all got involved trying to help and I remember thinking as I pushed a trolley full of books, with Harry Newman ahead of me, "This is a funny way to manage a company!" But it did work in the end and has grown to what it is today.

The most important development during my time at Wiley Ltd was the acquisition of the Heyden journals. Mike Foyle received the original approach from Gunther Heyden and I then had to organise the long period of courtship and make sure it happened. We knew early on that we wanted these mature and successful titles, but we had to convince New York that it was a good idea and Gunther that he really did want the cash. The deal was completed just about the time I transferred to New York, in May 1982. The turnover of Wiley Ltd was then about £8 million and with the Heyden journals the profitability of the operation was transformed.

My transfer to New York as Vice President and General Manager of the International Group was like going through the looking-glass—in more ways than one! I had to face up to the problem of getting the best out of companies of very varying sizes at different stages in their development, and with very different cultures—a fascinating task. There was also the problem of dealing with the perception among some of the US company staff that the International Group was simply an export department. With Brad Wiley as Chairman, with his intense enthusiasm for all things international, this might have seemed unnecessary, but there was still a hard core to be tackled. In fact more than half of the International Group's business derived from original publishing. Wiley Ltd continued to contribute at least half of this and, with the growth in journal business, became increasingly profitable. In spite of various difficulties, both external and internal, the international share of the corporation's total business was more than maintained during the six years I was in New York.

I was succeeded in Chichester by Mike Foyle in 1983, after an interim year during which Charlie Stoll acted as Managing Director. He had held a number of senior posts in the New York company before heading the International Group. He and I swapped places, and that it worked says a great deal for the personalities involved. Wiley were fortunate in Charlie Stoll, not only at that stage but later, when he was recalled to the board of John Wiley & Sons Inc., for he then played a key role in enabling the present senior management team of the parent company to evolve. I am glad to have had him as a colleague and friend.

When it was decided in 1988 to alter the structure of Wiley business outside the United States, Wiley Ltd absorbed a number of the functions of the International Group. Wiley Ltd has grown immensely since those days when I joined twenty years ago, but not out of all recognition. It is still a quality operation. Long may it remain so. I am proud to have had the chance of taking part.

SMALL WAS BEAUTIFUL: WILEY IN THE 1970s

Renée Southwell (Wiley 1969–1995)

I joined Wiley in 1969, when all the departments were under one roof in the Baffins Lane building, with the exception of the warehouse, which was on the industrial estate run by Gibbings Harrison. In the words of the old song, "Was it all so different then?" Well, yes, it was. Everyone knew everyone else by sight as well as by name. My salary for part-time work was £6 per week and we were all paid in cash. Marion Fisher would walk to the bank, accompanied by Bert from the Post Room, and bring back the cash for the wages in a shopping bag. (With inflation and the increase in staff she would need a wheelbarrow now.) Then, seated at her desk in a room full of people, with notes and coins all around her, she would make up the pay packets. When the management wanted to bring in payment by cheque there was considerable resistance, one member of staff refusing to budge until the bitter end.

I started in Customer Service, where orders were coded by hand using large metal tubs beside our desks. These tubs held cards in slats giving title, author and ISBN. We processed the orders by entering the ISBN and quantity on a form which was then passed to punch operators; from there the invoice was produced.

We had some great characters in Marketing. Chappie Chapman, a home sales rep, was always high-powered when phoning in his orders. We would pick up the phone to hear Chappie barking at us, "Got a pencil and paper ready? OK, here's the order," and woe betide if you kept him waiting. Ove Steentoft, then a rep, and now so sadly missed—what a raconteur and wit he was, with his tales of being mugged while on the job, having his belongings stolen, and, on one occasion, finding a hotel in Nigeria so below standard that he spent the night in an armchair in the garden. John Wilde, also a rep, told of being given a bucket of water for his ablutions, as the water supply was off, apparently a frequent problem in Nigeria, not to mention the phones and electricity also often being cut off, preventing all contact with the office sometimes for days on end. They all went that extra mile for Wiley in those early days. Mike Foyle, the Export Manager, often entertained booksellers or their children, anxious to learn English, in his own home, such was the rapport he had with his customers. I have memories of Mike riding to work on his rusty bike, a real old boneshaker, even when he became MD, on one especially memorable occasion holding aloft a large golf umbrella as he pedalled slowly along. No A27 bridge then and much less traffic!

Did we make mistakes? Of course we did. John Wilde told us of a small German bookseller in a quiet back street being confronted with a lorry unloading several boxes of books. He rushed out to stop them, to discover that his order for 20 text books had somehow become 200.

After writing ISBNs day in, day out, I decided I needed a change, so I went to Mike Foyle's department as an assistant secretary. It was part of my job to open and distribute the post for Export, but as the company grew this took longer and longer, especially when staff refused to accept letters not personally addressed to them, so the Post Room was asked to open and sort the post. This was not an unreasonable request, one might think, but it caused mayhem in the Post Room, as they did not consider it part of their job, and two people resigned.

Tea and coffee were not always freely available. We had two tea ladies, and drinks were brought round on a trolley trundling a huge tea urn (the tea definitely stewed if you were the last to be served). Two cups were the limit and the cupboard in the kitchen was locked in the lunch hour, so no nipping in there for an illicit cuppa! When the tea ladies left, Mr Newman was forced to issue a warning about the excessive amount of coffee being used; can't imagine that happening now!

Since those days and, maybe, due to the efforts of those first members of staff, Wiley has become a great success, well respected and admired by both academics and booksellers, who see Wiley as cast iron in its reliability and holding its position at the top of the league for quality of product. However, there was a time when all this was put in jeopardy when the whole company was brought to a halt for two weeks. This was during the miners' strike of '72. We had had continual strikes—buses, trains, hospital porters, dustmen—and when the miners dug in we were frequently plunged into darkness and left shivering without heat. Towards Christmas that year things got really bad, so the Directors decided to close until after the New Year.

This event also brought small but significant changes to Wiley. Until those dark cold days it had been an unwritten rule that women did not wear trousers to the office, and none did. (I can hear hoots of glee from my readers, but I warned you it was different then.) The first woman to break this rule was our receptionist. Reception was upstairs at the middle front door in Baffins Lane, and this door was usually open to enable visitors to walk up to reception. However, this made it very cold for the person sitting at the top of the stairs, so on went the trousers. Others quickly followed suit and it soon became quite acceptable.

To make this area near the front door more attractive there were several large plants just inside the door, with a sign indicating that reception was upstairs. We were amazed one day to see that the largest of these plants had disappeared, and wondered how the thief had managed to stagger up the road carrying the plant in its heavy pot.

We did not have the speed and convenience of new technology, but we got the job done. Sometimes staff within Marketing would join together to get a job done, leaving their other work. When Promotion had lots of envelopes to stuff and were overwhelmed we would sit round the table together, stuffing envelopes to beat the post.

One of my famous faux pas occurred at this time when I was asked to type a memo concerning mail to Nigeria which had to go "full rate", as second-class mail was ending up in the swamp. I tore off the memo and passed it to my manager without reading it. He passed it back to me, indicating that I had hit the key next to L, which is K, giving the word "full" an entirely different meaning. Red-faced, I took the awful piece of work back as he said with a twinkle in his eye, "Shouldn't that be for French letters?". Yes, we laughed a lot and it all seemed much less serious and desperate than now. We were a team and small *was* beautiful.

CHAPTER THREE

Selling and Marketing Around the World

OUR MAN IN THE NORTH 1972–1977

Stefan Usansky (National Accounts Manager)

AFTER WHAT seemed like a lifetime in academic bookselling—actually only ten years after allowing for remission for good behaviour—I responded to an advertisement in the trade press to join John Wiley & Sons Ltd as sales representative for "the North." So it was that in November 1972 I gave up a steady nine-to-five office job for a "Monday-to-whenever" career on the road, for an annual salary of £1,600 a year—and no bonus!

"The North", it transpired, actually consisted of the whole of the Midlands and the North of England, Scotland, Wales and Ireland! Only the Pope had a larger diocese. Whereas today the company has ten sales reps, in 1972 there were just two of us to cover the whole of the British Isles.

Despite the size of my territory (or maybe because of it) I did actually enjoy life on the road, travelling 50,000 miles a year in my Ford Cortina, especially as in those days I was given a new car every 30,000 miles or after one year, whichever came first! Even driving through snow and fog to visit a bookseller in Aberdeen to obtain a paltry twenty-unit order, or sitting in a two-hour traffic jam on the M6 (yes in 1972) was fun compared with serving students in a bookshop.

Life in those days was different from what it is today. We had a Labour government, we were only just getting to grips with decimalisation and we were still independent from the Common Market, as it was then known. And Manchester United had George Best, Denis Law and Bobby Charlton banging in goals from all angles. Paradise!

Contrary to popular belief, we work very hard at Sales Conferences (Villefranche 1990)

Selling books for Wiley was much easier a quarter of a century ago: libraries and students had "spend money". And computers were very much a thing of the future, so no bookshop in the country had a computer section. Indeed, we had only one computer book on our list, McCracken's *Guide to Fortran IV Programming*, which at the time was considered to be a high-level computer science title! We had no business or management books, no finance, popular science or law books—just expensive STM and college textbooks. For a trade rep, they really were the good old days.

Repping has also changed. In the 1970s the Net Book Agreement was still firmly in place, which meant that books were never sold at discount and as a result there was no pressure from my customers for extra discount or extended credit. Terms of 30%, 30 days, were considered to be very fair and were accepted without argument. There were no independent library suppliers and, apart from W.H. Smith, no wholesalers. So again, pressure for extra discount did not exist.

Also, twenty years ago books did not have ISBNs or bar codes. Teleordering, the fax machine and EDI were unheard of, so all ordering was done by sending orders through the post. There was no pressure on publishers to supply "by return". Indeed, 14-day delivery was considered to be "gold star" service. And most publishers supplied "firm sale only" so the frustrations which we have today with "returns" did not exist.

Jim Durrant's retirement (1981)
Top table from left to right: Charlie Stoll, Mrs Wiley, Jim Durrant, Brad Wiley Snr, Mrs Durrant

"Over to you"—Jim Durrant and Stefan Usansky

"On yer bike"—Jim Durrant and Shirley Howard

Two decades ago all bookshops were family owned. None of the major chains—Blackwells, Dillons or Waterstones—existed, whereas today they account for over a third of the total UK turnover. There were no head offices to negotiate with, so the pressures—to "contribute" to advertising in the press or on television, on the London underground, or on the sides of buses, or to take full-page advertisements in their magazines, or to "support" them (financially, of course) at freshers week, or to pay extortionate amounts for window displays—did not exist. Today we are expected to do all these.

When we look back at our schooldays all we remember is that during the summer holidays the sun always shone, even in Manchester. It was always the "good old days". And today, as I look back at my quarter of a century of selling books for Wiley, I can remember only the good times. Of course there was the odd "buyer from hell" but thankfully they were few and far between. Today there is less room for the eccentric. There were more "characters" in the trade in those days.

There was the major university bookshop run by a retired RAF commander who was so drunk by the end of the day, every day, that it took him at least three attempts, taking at least an hour, to cash up. On my visits I was expected to stay behind at 5.30 to "help" and, because the cash never tallied with the till receipts, we often had to go through the whole exercise at least three times. When, finally, the till roll and the cash actually matched we, naturally, had to celebrate—with a drink.

I also recall the bookshop which I didn't actually see for over a year because the manager, who insisted on doing all the buying himself, refused to look at the books in my bag anywhere other than in the pub. This was no problem, though as the orders increased in size in direct correlation with the quantity of beer he drank. I, naturally, stuck to Diet Coke.

Then there was the shop manager who insisted that we start business with a drink—not tea or coffee (it was, after all, only 9 a.m.), but a whisky from the bottle which she had hidden under her desk. Her welcome was always the same "Hello Stefan. Nice to see you. Will have tea, coffee or a drink?" When I suggested that coffee might be a good idea she responded by saying that she had no milk, so it had to be something a little stronger!

And I remember the police once being called to stop a brawl in the street outside a bookshop—one of my buyers was fighting with a customer!

Then there was the bookseller who invited my sales manager and me to his palatial house one day in the middle of a very hot summer so that we could all sit in comfort in his garden over a few drinks and together compile the autumn text book stock order in readiness for the following academic year. My boss told me to bring my swimming trunks as the outdoor swimming pool would be available. Wrong. My customer and my boss did indeed swim and drink (plenty of both), but I had to sit in the shade to write out the order whilst they enjoyed themselves. I never did get into the pool and what's more I had to chauffeur my boss home.

Funny how most of my stories revolve around drink!

A BOOKSELLER REMEMBERS

Stuart Johnston of John Smith & Son, Glasgow

Halliday and Resnick. Squat and oversized for any pocket, the first university text book I remember. Of course, I don't have it now; I sold it secondhand after that early 1960s physics course. But what I remember about it is curious. I remember the black colophon on the spine. The simple intertwined JW featured two of my initials: why hadn't the company used the S of John Wiley & Sons in its colophon? I could have stolen it, copied it onto the spine of all my books.

That early impression was still with me a few years later when, having learned that the book trade revolved around bookselling, and having arrived in the Goods In section of John Smith & Son in Glasgow, I found myself unpacking box after box featuring my favoured colophon. It was always a satisfactory experience, for even in those days packing varied enormously, and Wiley books, like most American imports, were now large-format, getting heavy, and had a satisfying user-friendliness.

Soon after, in our International Library Supply department, I learned another side of Wiley: customer service. Many American publishers used agents of one kind or another in the United Kingdom; others had offices which were conceptual extensions of the USA. John Wiley had set up an organisation which spoke to and listened to its customers. Jim Durrant was already a well-known name to Jimmy Hogg, then our Technical Department Manager, of course, but what made him stand out from other publishers was his evangelism on behalf of his customers. Nothing was too much trouble, for booksellers at any level; he was always happy to share with us his thoughts on how we might develop our customer base together, both at home and abroad.

This effective subliminal advertising for his company was to reap benefits in myriad ways, many of which continued to accrue over the subsequent years, indeed to this day, and distanced Wiley from its competitors. The stablility and reliability of Jim, and later Stefan Usansky, in the Sales Office stand in stark contrast to the ever-changing sales managers of rivals. It wasn't that Wiley didn't make mistakes; it was just that they were better at fixing the consequences. In all the little ways that STM booksellers subconsciously make positive decisions about subscriptions, about stock, about exhibitions, about window displays, about co-operative ventures, the name of John Wiley was always present, and correct.

Hidden to begin with, since Chichester—a synonym for John Wiley—acted as agency for a number of smaller US presses, the embryo of a British publishing programme began to emerge. Always elegantly produced, the books soon had a clear house style. I remember a local lecturer in civil engineering, David Clarke, approaching me in our Technical department with a completed typescript of *Computer Aided Structural Design*, and asking me for suggestions for a possible publisher. It was obvious from a first inspection that it already looked like a Wiley book, so the choice made itself. It is difficult to believe that thirty years of British publishing has been achieved with so little fuss, so few fanfares, but such is my perception of the Wiley style. It would have been wrong, almost improper, to do it any other way. The reputation and character of a list are always made by the unusual, as well as by the predictable, although some are best glossed over, unmentioned, soon forgotten!

In the summer of 1985 John Jarvis talked to me about a book coming from a local academic in August. The author, Walter Sneader, wanted a launch party, but John and I felt that this unassuming lecturer was almost "too nice a guy", lacking the controversy which helps lift the publicity about a book. However, after a long consultation over a beer or two, we decided in favour. At the launch we sold 293 copies of *Drug Discovery*, at full price(!), to the 300 people who came. How very satisfying to know that being nice—whether you are publisher or author—can be combined with being a success. How very Wiley!

Publishing is a shifting phenomenon, and the future is a challenge for all of us. If John Wiley can maintain their track performance over the next thirty years, their customers will have few complaints.

WHEN MACDONALD'S WAS A CINEMA ...

John Wilson, Sometime Rep for the South of England, and various other job titles 1974–1991

It is always amazing just how easily the mind and the memory can be persuaded to step back over twenty years. A pleasant lunch with Clive Horwood and Peter Ferris during one of my infrequent returns to the south coast had reminded me that there was another "Wiley-in-Chichester" anniversary on the horizon. My first encounter with John Wiley came in the autumn of 1974. In those days, the entire Wiley UK trade sales force consisted of two reps. The irrepressible Stefan Usansky was covering the frozen North, and the job for the South of England, which had been held by a friend of mine, was going to become vacant.

Then, as now, the publishing grapevine was active. I was working as a trade rep for an Oxford-based publishing company whose chairman's antics were as bizarre as his final demise. The job itself was virtually identical to the one I was proposing to leave. The only difference was that the reputations of the two companies were as different as chalk and cheese. The opportunity to join a real publishing company was irresistible. I should have been interviewed by Jim Durrant, the doyen of UK sales managers, and at that time a legend in his own lunchtime. But sadly Jim was ill, so I was interviewed by Mike Foyle and Harry Newman, who, bless them, decided to hire me. I still have the job offer telegram somewhere!

The "territory" to be covered was the whole of the South of England from Bristol up to Norwich, including London and all the major university towns. In the mid-seventies, the Wiley list was predominately science based, so the shops called on were usually on a university campus. However, then as now, there were other key accounts in major cities. There were Foyles and The Modern Book Company in London. The Dillons Group consisted of the one shop in Gower Street. There was also the wonderfully anachronistic H.K. Lewis in Gower Street, whose entire stock control system was based on thousands of small white cards, on which was written the entire sales history of every book ever subscribed for or stocked by the shop.

The mileage to be covered was substantial, with more than a thousand miles a week being in no way unusual. As the cars of the seventies were nowhere near as reliable as their nineties counter-parts, it was felt prudent to change them at 30,000 miles. In my case, that was sometimes less then ten months. My local garage made sure I was on their Christmas card list! My first day at Wiley has three distinct and lasting memories. It was raining, hard; in fact for the first four or five visits I made to Chichester it rained. I finally got to meet Jim Durrant, my boss. I was standing in reception, which was then on the second floor of the original Baffins Lane building, and this figure, in carpet slippers, padded down the office to greet me. Jim had been suffering from gout, that most unsympathetic but painful of ailments, and to ease his discomfort was wearing slippers. My induction week was a blur. It was my first encounter with the perils of trading in the mighty US dollar. I was told, with great solemnity, that if sterling ever went below $2.68 we were in big trouble. It did, but we survived!

At the time, I was in the process of moving flats in London and, to ensure that none of the usual rep's post, especially the sample copies, went astray, I had given my parents' address, as a safe refuge and post box. I used to call in fairly regularly, so was a little surprised to get a call from my father asking when I was going to pick up "all these b... books", as he wanted to put his car in the garage. There was a small mountain of books waiting to be collected. Custom and tradition in the London book trade, stemming from the days when publishers' representatives wore bowler hats to visit customers, decreed that the buyer must see finished copies of each new title before they ordered it!

I was often to be seen carrying large piles of books up and down the stairs in Foyle's to the various departments. On one occasion I was stopped by the store detective, who took a little persuading that I was not stealing my own sample copies. Jim was a firm but fair taskmaster, and there were times when he liked and demanded a rapid response from "his boys". Periodically, he would go through the computer printouts, which listed little more than the names and addressed of customers who had purchased books, especially new customers buying from us for the first time. Little notes would appear in the post: "When are you next in Plymouth?", "Reading is worth a visit", "Go and see this man in Cambridge," and so on. Enough to say that these calls upon my time became more and more strident, as I stubbornly refused to be deflected from big shops in big towns, who placed big orders!

Finally, under protest, I gathered up all the outstanding "What about Colchester?" notes and set off to spend the week, boldly going where no rep had gone before. I think it was my report of the visit to a chicken farm in Peterborough that finally stopped the "What about?" notes, or it might have been the church in Reading. The computer in those days was quite unable to distinguish between different sorts of customers, and you got details of everybody who purchased a single book!

After a couple of years on the road, which included the blistering summer of 1976 (who can forget the joys of PVC car seats in hot weather?), I was finally hauled "off the road" and into the office, where they could keep a proper eye on me. Then, as now, John Wiley was the company to emulate; its reputation for professionalism, hard work and sheer quality was the envy of all its competitors. The "Wiley way" was the way to do it. I did it for seventeen years, and look back on it from the wilds of Buckinghamshire with huge affection for the people, the town and the imprint. Thanks for the memories. Onwards to the next thirty years.

EARLY DAYS IN INTERNATIONAL SALES

Mike Foyle (former Managing Director 1983–1993)

1963 was a big year for Wiley's Europe sales: the one rep covering the Continent had just left, and the decision was taken to appoint two in his place: one for German-speaking countries and the North, which Ove got; the other for "Southern Europe". Southern Europe was defined as the area bounded by Paris/Athens/Palermo/Lisbon; this was to be mine. The then Yugoslavia was included, being regarded as just on our side of the Iron Curtain. Turkey and Israel were added later.

I could hardly believe my luck: I had been a schoolmaster, and I was now going to be given an expense account and paid for travelling to these places. In fact, my wife Margaret and I were soon

> ```
>                               7.7.69.
> MF.
>
> Dear Mike,
>         Encl. a letter from Klitgaard, Gjellerup plus some photos, which
> he took during our "conference" - I have permitted myself to give some
> captions on the back of some of the photos. Who - if any - should see
> these I leave to you to decide, but I think they are rather fun. The
> translation of Klitgaards letter is as follows:
>
>                 "... thank you for a delightful and useful afternoon. Encl.
>                 a few photos illustrating your "profit" from the afternoon.
>                 Best reg. etc....
>                 In haster the most hearty greetings -
>                 also to the lady in the house... "
>
>         Actually it was a most profitable afternoon - in spite of the
> swimming interlude - or perhaps even because of it - at least it proves
> the sort of terms on which we are with one of our important customers.
> I doubt whether the McGraw-H. people are ever photographed by their
> sutomers in a state of "un-dress".
>                                         yours sincerely
> ```

An early trip to Scandinavian booksellers

living on the territory itself. We were told to find somewhere within range of an airport, and the airport we chose was Nice. I told them it was never closed by fog. I did not tell them—till it was too late—that we were to live in a flat built into the wall of a Grimaldi fortress hill-village, with a sunny terrasse but no telephone.

There is something reassuring about having alps between you and your boss, if only the Alpes Maritimes; to be without a telephone was an additional bonus. Fax didn't exist of course, and the nearest phone was a hundred metres away, up a cobbled street at Jimmy's Bar on the Place Grimaldi. A waiter would occasionally come down to summon me. At that time the French telephone system rivalled their loos as the worst in Western Europe, so even if you had a phone you might spend a long time getting through, and be inaudible when you did.

The terrasse, with its geraniums, bougainvillea, parasol and endless supplies of rosé on the rocks, made a good base office. Later we moved to Lake Como, where the terrasse was replaced by a garden and boathouse, and the rosé by Soave at a shilling a litre. In practice, I wasn't at base much: I travelled three weeks in every four, often without getting back at weekends. Mostly, though, Margaret was able to come with me. Once we did a seven-week trip. We went by car, a Fiat 1500. UK reps had Austin

The risks and dangers of discussing problems with Scandinavian booksellers

MF and OS *facing the problem*

1100s at the time, and I persuaded my boss that this large engine was necessary for the long Continental distances. We ate modestly and stayed in cheap hotels, and developed a list of those where a double room cost the same as a single. I would visit the accounts in a town while Margaret's job was to find some parking and wait till I reappeared. Waiting often involved fending off attentions at places like the Trevi fountain, the Ritiro, or on the beach at Tel Aviv. I wrote up reports in longhand, and she would type them up on a portable typewriter. When we had finished a particular town, the reports would all be put in an envelope together with the claims, requests for returns, excuses for late payment, orders for leaflets and catalogues, and the occasional order for books, and put in the post before we set off for the next town. Italy used to take four weeks, and the seven-week trip involved carrying on by ferry from Brindisi to Patras, where we were woken by donkeys, up from Athens into Bulgaria (passing through a military border which had been opened only days before, and at one point narrowly avoiding a herd of wild horses), and from Sofia to Belgrade; then home via Zagreb, Liubliana, Trieste and Milan, including Venice for the weekend of course.

I had the benefit of excellent mentors: Jim Durrant, wise, generous, humane; the brilliant Mike Colenso, Sales Manager at twenty-four; and the incomparable Ove Steentoft. Mike took me to meet the key booksellers in Paris, Florence and Rome, showed me how to entertain important customers and told me how he judged a hotel room by the number of its lights (in Rome, the

John Wilde in Ibadan in the 1970s. John was Sales and Marketing Director in the 1980s and left the company in 1989. Mike Foyle announced John's departure as follows: "John Wilde, after 17 years of working with me (when I was export sales manager, I took him on as my assistant manager), is leaving to do his own thing. I shall miss his strong analytical mind, his reliability, and his unshakable personal integrity." Nowadays, John and Traute Wilde run their own freelance agency and represent Wiley in Germany, Austria and Switzerland.

Mike Foyle visits our agents in Nigeria, Spectrum Books

rooms we stayed in each had twenty-four). He also took me to Barcelona, Madrid and Lisbon, but after that I was on my own.

I started with France. I was asked (or perhaps I suggested it) to try investigating the potential of the provinces. Thus began the first of many agreeable weeks probing the sales possibilities for American scientific books in Nancy and Nantes, Bordeaux and Besançon, Marseilles, Aix and Montpellier. It was more congenial than Paris, where almost all the business came from; Parisian booksellers were highly professional and unforgiving to an inexperienced rep. We had just installed a new computerised order-processing system, and it threw everything into chaos for the whole of 1964. I would note the list of blunders and dutifully report them back to London, then three months later I would call in again and hear that nothing whatever had been done. I was petrified of some of those booksellers. With really tough ones like the formidable M. Emard of Offilib, I used to take Margaret in with me to smooth my passage. It didn't correct the errors, but otherwise it worked wonders; they were always gallant when she was there. 1964 was a rough apprenticeship year, but I always felt it was a very useful experience. It convinced me that you had to get the back office systems really right before you bothered with sending reps out, and I never forgot how lonely a rep can sometimes feel out there.

A meeting of the International Group in the early 1980s—Dennis Hudson, Mike Foyle, Adrian Higham, Jamie Cameron, Bob Hauck, Marianne Orlando, Charlie Stoll, Harry Newman, John Collins, Dan Rubin and Tom Cassidy

There were many compensations. Over time I tried the Spanish provinces too, and the Portuguese, Swiss, Belgian and Greek. I once conceived a plan to investigate every Mediterranean island, and had designs on Mallorca, Cyprus, Crete and Rhodes, but after Sardinia, Sicily and Malta the plan foundered and I never completed it. My biggest single achievement in sales pioneering was to set up a standing order with a bookseller in Venice. It was only for one copy in one subject, but on the theory that great oaks from little acorns grow, I tended it lovingly and visited often, and so did my successors.

At least, my immediate successor, David Trimmer-Smith, did. He, I could clearly see, was destined for greater things: having chosen a Swiss ski resort as his base, and having persuaded us that he should improve his Italian, he sent in bills for tuition, which we duly paid, only later discovering that the tutor was an Alitalia air stewardess he was living with. He used to breeze into our offices in Victoria through the drizzle in, say, February, suntanned, single and with lightweight suit, spend a couple of days dazzling the women in the office, then shoot off to Israel or somewhere, leaving us all thoroughly disgruntled. (David became Vice President with OUP New York, and, sadly, was in the Lockerbie air crash).

On the subject of standing orders, there were French and Italian booksellers who would take five or ten copies in every subject, and most of them got sold. And in Yugoslavia there was a wonderful financing scheme called IMG. American taxpayers' money was made available to Yugoslav book importers for the purchase of American books. We had a thing called the Staple Stock List which contained virtually every book we published. At the annual Belgrade Book Fair, booksellers would go through it putting 2s and 3s against almost every title (including sets of Kirk-Othmer) to use up their IMG allocations.

Once, driving homeward out of Belgrade after the Fair, we stopped to buy pickles. My briefcase was stolen, and with it every list with every order I had taken. A lot of things go through a rep's mind on such an occasion, and in my case, through his bowels as well. I finally decided there was nothing for it but to spend a couple of days revisiting every bookseller, wipe the egg from my face, and confess. The story actually had a happy ending. There were still a lot of IMG dollars swilling about and booksellers were glad to find something to use them on. I actually ended up with bigger orders than I had originally.

Our UK publishing was only just starting, and at Wiley, journals were unheard of. We were all-purpose reps, textbook and trade, but we were selling American books only. They were hardback, heavy, luxurious things, and the textbooks were expensive for Europe. Somebody at McGraw Hill thought up ISEs, and after a lot of analysis and heart-searching we followed suit with WIEs, being told we had to sell at least 80 per cent more units to make the scheme work. As I recall, we did this easily, and they worked wonderfully well in Nigeria and Kenya too—but that is another story.

OVE STEENTOFT: A TRIBUTE (1995)

Bob Long (Sales and Marketing Director)

Ove Steentoft joined Wiley in early 1963 and represented us for over thirty years in various parts of the world. His initial responsibility was for northern and eastern Europe, and whilst these territories had already been opened up for Wiley by others, his contribution was to develop our position to one of market leadership and immense prestige. Ove went on to cover southern Europe and Nigeria and, in the late 1970s, transferred to Wiley in New York in order to cover the Middle East, where he once again encountered the kind of demanding but stimulating markets he had enjoyed working in previously. He returned to work for Wiley Europe when we assumed responsibility for coverage of the Middle East in 1988. In the past two years he has resumed coverage of Pakistan on behalf of Wiley in Singapore, with spectacular success.

Foreign travel was nothing new to Ove when he joined Wiley. He had already lived for several years in Nigeria, where he met and married his wife, Margaret, whilst working for Evans Brothers and Cambridge University Press. Upon the family's return to the UK, Ove joined the University of London Press and travelled widely in Latin America and the Middle East. Ove's affection for this country (which began during his wartime experiences in the Danish resistance, including a long period of harsh imprisonment) prompted him to come here.

Work and travel were integral and inseparable components of Ove's life. He was happiest when abroad, especially at book fairs, where he had an uncanny ability to forget the names of the people he was dealing with, but was yet able to extract either large orders or large amounts of money owed to us, depending on what was called for. He was an indefatigable champion of customers when he came up against "piffling" bureaucratic obstacles within the company. He believed that customers should be treated with skill, integrity, and style—principles that were as valid at the end of his career as they were at the beginning.

Ove's salesmanship and colourful personality gave a lot to the company, but his other great contribution was the development of successive generations of younger colleagues to whom he generously passed on his expertise. He was a great raconteur who enjoyed deeply the company of good friends over a good dinner. He believed that the intensity of life was more important than its duration by far. I am glad that my only memories of Ove will be of the man enjoying his life to the full, and I am sure he would not have wanted to leave us in any other way.

OVE'S FALCON EPISODE

Ove Steentoft

One of the many hazards of travelling in the Middle East is the likelihood of an aeroplane breaking down in midflight, a hazard I experienced on my way to Bahrain. Such hazards many of us experience. But this particular hazard was followed by yet another—and to me novel—vicissitude, which perhaps few of my colleagues have had the pleasure of.

Having taken off from Karachi in the evening—en route to Bahrain via the Sheikdom of Qatar—on a GF Tristar, we managed to get about twenty minutes' flying time out of Karachi, when the captain announced, "Please do not panic. There is no reason for panic, and I am sure we will get down, but the flaps don't work at all, and I am returning to Karachi, hoping to land and get the flaps repaired". After half an hour's more flying—all the while contemplating this most comforting and encouraging statement from the pilot—we did actually land, after a fashion! However, no one was hurt.

When we came to a standstill, I was offered the chance of boarding another, but rather small, plane, which was due to take off in half an hour's time, also destined for Bahrain. I seized this chance and was rushed in a car across the tarmac. An airline official grabbed my ticket and ran into the offices to have it re-assigned, while I was hurried on board and into the small cabin, where only one seat was left. The airline very kindly gave this to me. In the rush, of course, I never got my ticket back, and in the confusion I forgot to ask for this quite useful document.

After a few minutes the rest of the passengers started boarding. I was indeed honoured, because they were all of them princes from the Sheikhdom of Qatar, with an entourage of falconers. They brought with them their 79—repeat 79—falcons—all on falcon sticks wearing dainty little leather masks over their pretty but vicious-looking faces. There were placed wherever there was any space in the cabin. Hence I had seven falcons under my feet, four above my knee, one by my left arm, and four above my head. Although the falcons did have these lovely little masks over their faces, they had no masks or "containers" fastened to their nether ends! Need I comment further on what this resulted in? The falcons were rather nervous and reacted violently by perpetually dispensing with what had become superfluous matter in their stomachs!

After 15 minutes the somewhat distraught stewardess asked me if I would like to—somehow or other—extract myself from what had by then become an entanglement of dozens of, though very expensive, nevertheless vicious-looking and rather too generous (in a fluid sort of manner) winged friends. I very readily agreed and managed to extract myself from my imprisonment in this most princely aviary. I was then offered accommodation next to the pilot, in the small space allotted to the stewardess. The stewardess happened to be allergic to birds—even to princely birds! Hence it was a while before, at the captain's most reasonable suggestion, I was able to avail myself of the toilet facilities of the plane. When both the stewardess and I had managed to attend to our different ablutions, we both collapsed on the floor choking with unquenchable laughter.

Some three hours later we landed in Doha, where the princely princes and their most precious and most generous winged friends left the plane. A whole army of cleaners boarded the plan to "tidy" it up after the departure of the princely passengers—and a whole army was needed, and much profit was made by some disinfectant factory! The stewardess left the plane, and was not seen again. We flew off without her.

INTERLUDE FOR DANE, ENGLISHMAN, AND TWO LUNATICS

The scene is the first floor office in Barcelona of Señor X an occasional purveyor of Wiley books. [Ove Steentoft] OS and [Peter Lawson] PL enter left, discovering X involved with one of five telephones on his desk; at opposite end of room sits Y, behind the remaining six telephones. Somewhere between sits pretty secretary, who at irregular intervals during ensuing conversation collapses prettily over typewriter, apparently helpless with laughter.

With unusual speed, OS recognises and puts a name to Y, who rises, and they make their way towards each other through the familiar debris of lunatic mail order booksellers. Mezzoforte pleasantries are exchanged, PL tempted to suggest Danish as acceptable median language, but holds tongue.

After some minutes Señor X finishes phone conversation,

which was evidently long distance [*fortissimo*], and lowers his decibel count slightly to greet OS and PL. New conversation develops as follows:

SEÑOR X: Slidgeworthy grimble mucho loch ness sprocket brackle gungle.
Y: Señor X, ee say, slidgeworthy grimble mucho loch ness sprocket brackle gungle.
OS: Uh huh [*noncommittal, but positive*].
[PL *pretends to look for valuable heirloom which has just fallen on to floor*]
SEÑOR X: [*crescendo ma non rallentando*] Gramble no chistockle penguin [*beams broadly at OS*].
Y: Señor X, ee say, Gramble no chistockle penguin.
OS: Ah, I see, no, of course not.
[PL *drops another even more priceless heirloom*]
SEÑOR X: [*ff, crescendo, accelerando*] Gibber.
Y: Señor X, ee gibber.
OS: Mm, of course.
[PL *decides floor is best place to be*]
SEÑOR X: [*sf, accelerandissimo*] } Parlez-vous français?
Y: } ¿Habla Vd. frances?
OS: } Say something that makes sense.
[PL *recognises civilised language and finds heirloom*].
ALL: [*sff crescendissimo, in varying degrees of French*] Slidgeworthy grimble mucho loch ness sprocket brackle gungle.
OS: Uh huh, yes, yes.

Now a medium for communication has been established, and the previously cordial but unspecific discussion can be steered towards business matters. Señor X [*fff*] expresses surprise at and disappointment in our practice of not crediting returns sent back to Chichester in paper egg cartons and marked "Not Known at This Address". OS and PL point to the 1,719,423 letters from SB on the subject, which draw attention to the advantages of applying a postage stamp to something being sent by post. Señor X [*ffff*], an admirable traditionalist, explains indignantly that his system has been proved over many years of exhaustive tests.

PL [*f*] comments postal service not as quaintly reliable as they used to be. Señor X says he has been doing it for 12 years.

Y: Señor X ee say ee do it from a undred years.

PL [*ff*] points again to unreliability of such a system.
Señor X says he has been doing it for 12 years.
PL rediscovers benefits of dropping valuable heirloom.
OS seeks to maintain sanity with massive nicotine injection.
Señor X, loyally interpreted by Y, explains he has been returning books in this way for some time now.
PL gives up hunt for heirloom and kicks table over, dropping valuable desk calculator on to floor.
OS finds interesting wallpaper at far end of room.
Sound of many typewriter keys being pressed simultaneously, as pretty secretary collapses over keyboard.
Y punches some figures into the dropped calculator, ostensibly to make sure it is still working, but in fact to discover increase in capital outlay caused by putting stamps on envelopes. Says something to Señor X in colloquial Spanish.
Señor X blanches, drops to fff, protesting weakly he has been using this system for some time now.

SEÑOR X: (in Spanish)	Blicklefuge!
Y: (in French)	
OS: (in Danish)	No Blicklefuge!
PL: (in English)	

Agreement thus being seen to be reached, OS and PL cut losses and run to waiting taxi, whose driver had previously expressed concern at seeing the words "Instituto Psiquiatrico del Estado" over the front door (meaning "Wiley books on sale here").

OS and PL pursued downstairs by Y apologising [*ff*] "Je m'excuse, je m'excuse", tapping his head with one index finger and pointing up at Señor X's office with the other.

JUNGLE WARFARE AT WILEY

John Lea (Marketing)

On Monday 26th June 1972 I joined Wiley. *Richard Nixon was still President of the USA but just nine days earlier on Saturday 17th June 1972 there had been a minor burglary at the Watergate complex in Washington and five men were arrested at 2:30. The rest is history.* I had come from the battlefields of Vietnam to the jungle warfare of Wiley. In those days the feuds between Marketing and Editorial were almost as exciting as the war itself. While the Americans in Vietnam were obsessed by the daily body count of enemy dead, others in Wiley were obsessed by a similar "numbers game"—How many leaflets? How many addresses? How many advertisements? How many inserts? Jamie Cameron, Editor for business, finance and engineering (and later to become Editorial Director) was every bit as formidable as the Vietcong and just as I grew to respect the cunning determination of the Vietcong I grew to respect the forward-thinking strategy and professionalism of Jamie Cameron. He built a magnificent list of books and an even better list of highly successful and profitable journals. Jamie may have been the "enemy" in those days but his legacy continues and every year when we rely on those early journals to deliver our sales targets we should raise a glass to him.

My first two years with Wiley were as Assistant Promotion Manager working for Alan (ASH) Hawes. The responsibility of the Assistant Promotion Manager in those days included the fulfilment of our Chichester journal—yes, just one—*Numerical Methods in Engineering*. All subscriber names and addresses were maintained on Scriptomatic cards which carried a carbon copy of the address and would last for about a dozen mailings before needing renewal. Indeed all of our mailing list was maintained on Scriptomatic cards—booksellers, libraries and individuals.

We attempted to separate promotion into two parts—"below the line" and "above the line". The principle being that all books received basic, general promotion (below the line) which included general catalogue, subject catalogue, Preview, NBI card (see below), review copies and possibly some space advertising. Above-the-line promotion was reserved for the more important titles. This form of promotion included solo leaflets, cluster subject leaflets, specialist advertising and extensive review copy treatment. It was a fine line in differentiating "above" and "below" as we had very extensive series advertisements in all the major journals across every area of STM publishing. Some regarded series advertisements as "below" and others regarded it as "above". Trevor Sanderson was our media specialist responsible for advertisements, list rental, review and later the computerization of the mailing list. Much of our time was taken up launching all our new Chichester journals worldwide. Trevor and I started with our second journal *Software Practice & Experience*, then our third, *Earthquake Engineering* and so on.

The Preview was printed using the old-fashioned hot-metal letterpress process and Alan Hawes had devised an economical way

> # Wiley New Book Information
> JOHN WILEY & SONS LTD   BAFFINS LANE   CHICHESTER   SUSSEX PO19 1UD   ENGLAND
>
> *Medical Research*
>
> **HUMAN TUMOR MARKERS: Biological Basis and Clinical Relevance**
> edited by **H.E. Nieburgs, G.D. Birkmayer** and **J.V. Klavins**
>
> **Human Tumor Markers: Biological Basis and Clinical Relevance** is an in-depth look at the latest research on the value of tumor markers and new techniques for their detection. The book examines techniques for identification of human tumor markers to be utilized for detection, diagnosis, prognosis, and surveillance of cancer patients. Information on diagnosis and management of cancer according to site is presented in relation to the clinical utilization of carcinoembryonic antigen, tissue polypeptides, antigens derived from nucleic acid components, radioimmunoassay, hormones, receptors, and application of monoclonal antibodies. Topics of interest include tumor markers in tissue extracts; hormones as tumor markers; the recognition of human broncogenic carcinomas; lung tumor-associated antigens: thin layer immunoassay; clinical utility of different tumor markers in breast cancer and gynecological malignancies; surface antigens defined by monoclonal antibodies as tumor markers in human leukemia.
>
> *Readership:* Researchers and Clinicians working in the fields of Oncology, Biology, Pathology, Immunology, Embryology, Biochemistry, Pediatrics, and those working in Cancer Control and Cancer Research.
>
> 0 8451 0228 1   346pp   Jan'84 $77.40/£43.00
>
> *Published by Alan R. Liss, Inc., and marketed and distributed by John Wiley & Sons Ltd.*

New Book Information

of producing single title information pieces by using the identical Preview entries and transferring them onto little cards measuring $5\frac{3}{4}'' \times 4\frac{1}{4}''$. These were the legendary New Book Information (NBI) cards. In the 1960s, 1970s and early 1980s everyone from the Max-Planck Institute to the North Bersted milkman knew the NBI card. The academics used them for the correct reasons (we hope) while most Wiley staff used the reverse side for note pads, shopping lists, and of course notes for the local milkman. We printed them for the individuals on the mailing list, in bulk for booksellers and, after our journal programme developed, as inserts into every relevant Chichester journal. We printed millions. They were printed "8 up"—i.e. 8 different cards cut from the same sheet. Print numbers were rounded up for economies of scale and every month maybe 15,000 to 20,000 or more would be surplus to requirements—hence their use as note pads. We had massive electronic collating machines built that could sort combined sets of the cards. In our strongest subject areas an individual might receive up to 20 or 30 different cards per mailing.

31st May 1974 Alan Hawes resigned as Promotion Manager and *Richard Nixon was still President of the USA—but only by the skin of his teeth. A couple of months later at 11:35 a.m. on 9th August 1974 Nixon resigned.*

Meanwhile I took over as Promotion Manager for the next 10 years and the responsibilities were wide-ranging. We structured the department like an advertising agency with copywriters, graphic designers, media specialists, review specialists and of course the mailing room personnel who were responsible for collating, stuffing and mailing everything. In those days we were also responsible for all the company's recruitment through consultants and via space advertising—and we never used *The Guardian*!

We were promoting about 2,000 new books and launching about 5 or 6 new journals every year. In addition to approximately 1,000 new Wiley books we had a similar number of agency titles.

Philip Kisray looks much better since he had his wart removed! (Opening of Paris office)

Many of these came under the umbrella Halsted Press imprint—such publishers as Dowden, Hutchinson & Ross or Gardner Press. Halsted Press was a division of Wiley USA which offered smaller US publishers the opportunity to have European marketing, promotion and sales undertaken by Wiley Chichester. We needed the extra revenue generated by such sales as we had so few of our own titles. Very soon we represented other lists direct from the USA—such publishers as Ballinger, Jai Press and Ann Arbor Science. These were managed directly with the American publishers and not via Wiley Inc. We then went on to represent more local publishers—the best known being Ellis Horwood from our own small city. We were probably handling more new books then than we are now. We even had to compile our own general catalogue on a card index system because there were several thousand titles marketed by Wiley Ltd which were not in the Wiley Inc. catalogue.

The lists grew and grew until we were deluged with new books from all quarters and probably some of the Wiley titles suffered because they were being diluted or swamped by the hundreds of non-Wiley titles in our promotions. In 1982 we had a severe overstock situation with Wiley Chichester titles and decided on a massive "warehouse" sale. We organized an extensive campaign across every subject area where there were overstocks—everything from a 2 or 3 title niche campaign to large 120-plus title campaigns in Chemistry and Life Sciences. We gambled £30,000 promoting overstocks and managed to bring in sales revenues of over £100,000 (i.e. spending about £70,000 and bringing in about £230,000 at today's values). It was a very good return on investment with over three pounds back for every one pound spent—and nearly 100% of it direct from individuals as very few booksellers were involved.

Then in the spring of 1984 we had a major restructure—*and Ronald Reagan was now President!* In 1984 the Promotion Department was disbanded and split into four separate departments, each responsible for a major share of the business—textbooks, Chichester books and journals, New York professional and reference books and agency books. (Textbooks had always had their own department but now they were to undertake their own promotion.) I took responsibility for the Wiley New York titles—perhaps because I was so pro-American! My brief was to run a separate business and to regard all other books—even Wiley Chichester titles—as competition. They were exciting years and we had some tremendous new titles to promote and sell throughout Europe. They included Kirk-Othmer *Encyclopedia of Chemical Technology* third edition and the *International Dictionary of Medicine & Biology* (IDMB). This was the first major new medical dictionary in English to be published in 20 years. The publicity and sales campaign was so successful that European sales were outstripping those in the USA during the first six months. Never before had we had so much revenue from one title in so short a period. Sadly IDMB was to be sold a few years later along with Mandell's *Principles & Practice of Infectious Diseases* and Kirklin's *Cardiac Surgery*. Other key titles in this period included the first edition of the *Encyclopedia of Packaging Technology*—now successfully relaunched with a second edition in February 1997. During this period some young and very talented newcomers joined the (Chichester) New York professional and reference department. They were Sue Stewart, Sarah Stevens, Tony Carwardine and Philip Kisray and they made it an exceptionally strong team.

Then in late 1988 to early 1989 we had another restructure—*and George Bush was now President!* We amalgamated the Chichester, New York and agency marketing and promotion teams back into one group under the management of John Wilson. My role changed again and I took on responsibility for the marketing and sales of Wiley Inc. and Wiley Ltd books and journals into Japan. Wiley Inc. closed most of its international division and Wiley Chichester took on responsibility for Japan and our Tokyo office. Japan was a market similar to our own in terms of demand for high level STM books and journals. It was another exciting period. Our long-serving Tokyo Office manager, Hiroshi Tsukabe retired and we appointed Tadashi Hase as his successor—ably supported by Setsuko Saito as Promotion Manager. Sales increased—particularly for our European and American journals. Indeed some 80% of our Japanese sales revenue came from STM journals. During this period Wiley Chichester launched its first looseleaf laboratory manuals and *Cell & Tissue Culture* and *Preparative Biotransformations* were instant bestsellers through exclusive sales deals with the giant Maruzen company. A number of us enjoyed visits to Japan in the five-year Wiley Ltd stewardship. It was hard work, a unique culture but very rewarding. Stephen Smith joined Wiley in September 1992 as Vice President for Asia based in Singapore. But this time the rest of Asia was developing rapidly with massive growth in journal sales in South Korea and Taiwan and it made good sense for Wiley to have a regional Vice President managing the whole operation. So by December 1993 I withdrew from the Asian scene. *Bill Clinton was now President—but fortunately Bob Dole was still Senate Majority Leader!*

The new Direct Marketing Unit, established in 1995 under the leadership of Paul Holmes who joined Wiley from Mercury Communications. Pictured here are Michael Sherman, Melissa Cox, Nicky Christopher, Nicky Douglas, Dave Robinson, Alex Plowman, and (front row) Paul Holmes and Cheryl Williams

CHAPTER FOUR

Information Technology at Wiley, 1967–1997

Peter Ferris (IT Director)

I DOUBT that anyone would argue the logic of my being asked to write this section. Having been responsible for computers in Wiley UK for the whole thirty years I should be well placed to chronicle the changes that have taken place and the impact they have had on our business.

When we moved to Chichester from our London office we brought with us a collection of machinery which is now only to be seen in the Science Museum! Hard to believe that in the late sixties computers were still comparatively rate and extremely expensive beasts owned by large companies and utilities. They took up enormous amounts of space and required constant attention from engineers and technicians. Wiley was ahead of the field in those days because it had an IBM machine to handle invoicing and accounting. Many businesses of our size used addressing machines with metal plates for each customer address and posted all transactions manually into an accounting machine.

Wiley's first computer was in fact no computer at all. It went by the catchy name of IBM 444 tabulator and was a hideously ugly, fat, grey box about four feet high and six feet wide. As its name implied, it tabulated, but it could not compute! To compute you must be able to handle the four basic mathematical functions—add, subtract, multiply and divide—using a stored program. Our mechanical box could manage only to add and subtract, using noisy relays which clicked and clattered all day. There was apparently an extra-cost feature which gave it the capacity to multiply and divide, but this was considered unnecessary! Can you imagine running the whole business on a machine that could not multiply or divide?

It had no capacity for storing information or programs. Information went in and came out on cards in the form of holes. Programs telling it what to do with the information took the form of three foot square boards full of holes into which we plugged wires. Depending on where each end of the wire went the machine processed information on the cards and produced either print (it had its own built-in printing unit which went at a snail's pace) or more holes in more cards. We had a board full of wires for each application. Amazingly this all worked most of the time, but things could and did go wrong. Wires would fall out of their holes in the boards and we couldn't tell where they had come from, producing some strange results. Punched cards were easily and often dropped, and sequence was all-important. Sometimes cards would disappear inside the machine, only to reappear weeks later!

To support this card-eating, clanking monster we had an array of equally grey machines with equally sexy names—the 082 card sorter, which sorted cards into sequence; the 026 card punch, for punching holes into the cards in the first place; the 059 collator, for merging two decks of cards together; and the 007 summary punch, for punching new holes into cards as a result of a particular process. We employed four or five women who spent their entire day punching cards to create the data to be processed.

The Data Processing Department circa 1980 (note the flares!). Left to right: Debbie Hodge, not known, Brian Martin, Gwenda Keates, Di Southern, Peter Broadbridge, John Young, Jonathan Cox.

For invoicing we had pre-punched cards containing title code (in those days only five digits), description, price and quantity. Different coloured cards were used for different quantities. To "pull" an order you first selected the cards with the customer name and address, then a card for each title ordered. If a customer wanted three copies of the same book, two title cards had to be selected containing a one and a two quantity.

In those early days there were only three of us in the data processing department to look after the machines, plus the "punch girls" as they were affectionately called.

Not surprisingly, as the business grew in Chichester we realised that we could not continue with this machine. We needed to be able to program grater flexibility into our systems: we needed a *real* computer. Enter in 1970 the IBM 360/20: our first real computer that could store a program in its vast memory of 8k. It was still punch-card fed for both programs and data, but had a separate printer and an amazing unit called an MFCM—multi-function card machine. Some unkind people used to refer to it as the malfunctioning card machine, as it could be somewhat troublesome. It had two input stacks and five output stacks and cards could be read and punched in one pass. Not only that, but the cards passed through a 90 degree corner on their way through. An amazing machine which had to be seen to be believed.

With the help of some training in RPG, the new programming language, and Arthur Andersen, we developed a complete suite of new programs to run the business, since nothing could be transferred from the old machine. Ronnie Gorlin was the AA manager on the project. The changeover was a nightmare, but we survived. We still needed the sorter and collator and the card punches to process all the cards before and after they went through the computer. Still no disk or tape! Every piece of data held was in the form of holes in punched cards.

As we developed more complex programs the 8k memory just was not sufficient and had to be upgraded to a massive 12k. I remember feeling guilty about this and wondering if I was being too ambitious!

The 360/20 was at the bottom end of a family of machines which were inappropriate for our size of business, so in 1974 we migrated to a new range of IBM computers, the System 3 model 10. This was another leap forward in technology. Not only did it have a massive 16k of memory, it also had magnetic disk storage! Four disk drives, each with a 2.5 megabyte capacity, two of which had removable disks, enabling back-ups to be made and different disks loaded for each application. Punched cards were still the only input, through a 1442 card reader/punch. A typewriter console enabled the operator to enter commands to and receive messages from the computer. It used RPG2 as the programming language, an extension of the RPG introduced on the 360/20.

At the end of 1977 we moved the computer to the new distribution centre at Bognor, into a purpose-built room with air-conditioning and alarms.

In 1978 we moved to the biggest version of the System/3, the model 15. This was the first computer with a VDU console and the ability to run multiple tasks. It had significantly more memory, up to 256k, and larger disk capacity. We also added a tape drive for back-up. On this machine we developed our first on-line systems for order entry and enquiries, and gradually the job of the "punch girl" was eliminated. By 1982 all data entry was carried out by the originators, with no intermediate handling.

For this computer IBM introduced a new concept in disk storage, the Winchester disk. This was unique in that the read–write

---

Peter Ferris Celebrates 25 Years at Wiley

More than one hundred people gathered at the warehouse on September 21 to join Peter Ferris in celebrating 25 years at Wiley.

Members of staff were joined at the buffet reception by past Directors, Jim Durrant and Harry Newman. A "This is Your Life" presentation was made by Mike Foyle, who narrated the story of Peter's career at Wiley. Harry Newman recalled Peter's interview on joining Wiley with "school-boy's cap tucked in the back pocket of his shorts". Peter now looks forward to the 50-year long service award!

From left to right: Jim Durrant, Harry Newman, Peter Ferris and Mike Foyle

Grapevine 1990

heads were contained within the disk pack itself rather than being part of the drive mechanism. This enabled better sealing against contamination and greater capacity—70 megabytes per disk. Each disk weighed about 25 kilos, so you needed to be strong to lift them.

By the time we had perfected the System/3 IBM had talked us into moving to their latest family of computers, the System/38. This was another leap forward in technology, with memory now in megabytes, disk drives that could no longer be touched or seen, and a built-in database for the first time. From 1983 to 1988 we had a number of models of this series, culminating in the model 700. In 1986 we bought a second, smaller computer for the Baffins Lane office to spread our risk and overcome the problems of remote users. By 1988, however, we were outgrowing the capacity of this range and were relieved when IBM announced the AS/400 series, which quickly grew in power well beyond our needs.

In 1988 we installed an AS/400 B50 in Bognor and a year later added a B45 in Chichester. This machine was conceptually similar to the System /38 and the changeover was not too difficult, but the /400 gave us much improved performance and capability.

End of an era: Mike Foyle and Peter Ferris are pictured helping the System /38 computer on its way out of the door. In March 1990 the remaining 38 was replaced by the new IBM AS/ 400. The once-proud computer, which only days earlier had been supporting journals, accounts, editorial and marketing, had been reduced to a heap of spare parts.

In 1990 we decided to embark on the now famous Core system development, and introduced Synon as the application development tool. We installed the Core system in Singapore in May 1991 and later that same year in Australia. Our own system went live in May 1992. At the end of that year Eddie Russell, Steve Foster and Grant Burnett left us to work in New Jersey and developed the Core system for the parent company. This went live in October 1995, to complete the US transition to AS/400. Canada installed a version of the US Core system early in 1996. For the first time in its history Wiley was using the same computer technology in every location.

Also in 1990 the UK system took on the fulfilment of journals for Wiley USA and has continued to do so ever since. This system has been completely rewritten over the past three years and is about to take on fulfilment for VCH journals also.

In 1992 we installed a direct data and voice link between the UK and the USA and this link now carried all telephone and fax calls between the two companies, as well as allowing users at either end to access the remote AS/400s. In 1993 the link was extended to Canada and Colorado.

While all this was going on we also had to deal with the emergence of the personal computer and the workstation. In the late 1970s we had a few Apple II machines on which we ran simple word processing and the Visicalc spreadsheet program. I purchased the first IBM PC in 1980, with 64k of memory, no hard disk, no colour screen, for over £3,000! Slowly we introduced more PCs into the office, each with its own printer, as there was no network to connect to. Wordstar became the standard for word processing and remained so until the early 1990s. By the mid-80s the prices had come down and everyone had 20 or 40 megabyte hard disks. The first PC connections to the System /38 and AS/400 were made in 1987. As PC clones became acceptable we were able to buy colour screens, more memory and faster processors. 80286 machines arrived in the early 1990s, followed soon after by 386s, on which the first networks were based. Windows software began to be used in 1994 and is now the standard on all PCs.

Apple Macintosh computers were introduced in the early 1980s for design work in Production and Marketing, and their successors continue to be used. Our first Unix machines, called Apollo, came into Production in 1985 and were the forerunners of desk top publishing, which did not emerge until 1987/8. Our web site was launched in 1996 on a Sun workstation.

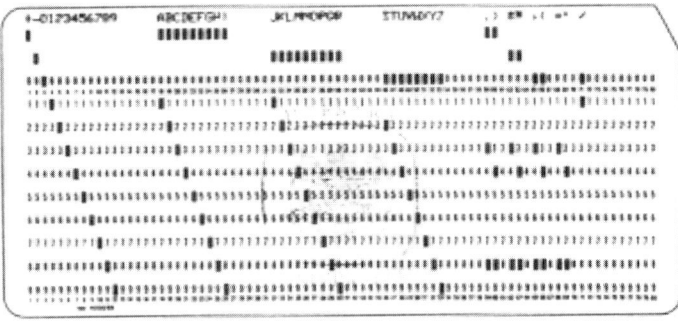

The punch card alphabet (a), and (b) a common keypunching device

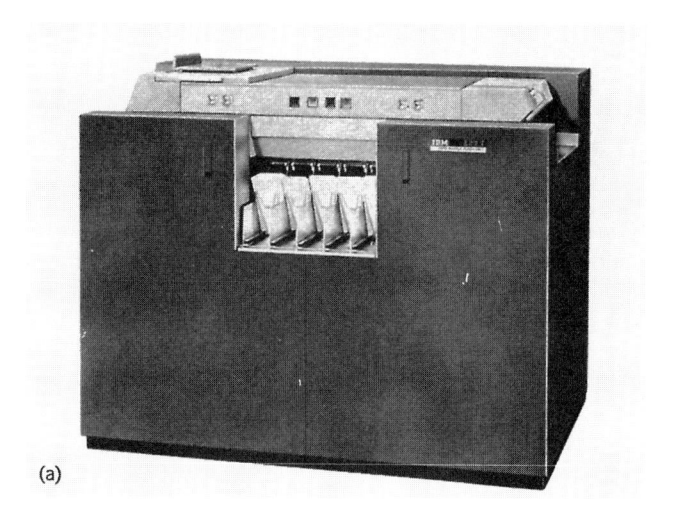

Input/output equipment in the IBM 1620 system: (a) 1620 Card Reader/Punch (b) 407 accounting machine

MAIN COMPUTERS AT WILEY CHICHESTER

1967	No memory, no disk, no terminals
1973	8k memory, still no disk, no terminals
1978	64k memory, 10 megabytes disk, still no terminals
1983	512k memory, 200 megabytes disk, a few terminals
1989	4 megabytes memory, 20 gigabytes disk, 200 terminals
1993	96 megabytes memory, 50 gigabytes disk, 250 terminals
1997	672 megabytes memory, 100 gigabytes disk, 350 terminals

CHAPTER FIVE

The 1980s

TWENTY-FIVE YEARS IN BRITAIN

AN EXTRACT from Jim Durrant's speech in 1985, celebrating twenty-five years since the company was set up in London:

We have come a long way during the last 25 arduous years. It has not been an easy road and we have caused our parent to produce cries of anguish, but also on the odd occasion a paternal slap on the back. From £150,000 in 1960 to £18 million in 1985, from 14 staff to 240, 20 word processors, 40 personal computers, and an Apollo system. It is believed that we are more advanced in the electronic and systems field than any other publisher in the UK, and possibly Europe. None of this would have been possible without the perception, fortitude and encouragement of Brad Wiley, Andy Neilly, Warren Sullivan and, in the background, the discerning eye of Esto Wiley. Equally, without the dedication of a loyal and hard-working staff, 90% of whom were new to publishing before joining us in Chichester, none of it would have been achieved, as it is only by teamwork that a publishing house can survive and prosper.

Obviously it is simply not possible to comment on every member of staff past and present, but the occasion should not pass without mentioning Tim Davies, our Financial Director, who has so ably steered us through a labyrinth of numbers which would have baffled Einstein; Peter Ferris, a real Londoner and just elevated to Director, who continues to guide us through an electronic maze with no visible exit; Messrs Dennis Fairs and Dennis Chaplin, who continue the endless production struggle; John Jarvis, Ian McIntosh, Ian Shelley, Peter Shepherd and others, looking for those elusive virgin publishing fields; John Wilde, coxswain of the marketing boat oared by Stefan Usansky; Bob Long, John Wilson, John

Promising lad—should go far (Bob Long 1982)

Lea and Lyn Udall; the band of secretaries, assistants, designers, etc., who make the whole thing tick; the accounts department and credit controllers, who so adroitly stop Marketing opening accounts in outer Mongolia, and so on. Lastly, but by no means least, a word about our vital distribution unit in Bognor, which took over from Gibbings Harrison and began operating in 1978. Its staff, despite the disruption caused by the recent installation of a mezzanine floor and mobile racking, processed 1.4 million books, and handled and recorded over 2,000 new title entries during the last year without impairing daily workflow. It was Stuart Bell who, with Yorkshire stubbornness and grit, knocked the warehouse together from 1967 to 1983, aided and abetted by the "hands and feet" of Charlie Snell, Bill Clinch, the allrounder Karin Davies in order processing, Wendie Westwood, and so many others.

CHARLIE STOLL

Jim Durrant wrote the following in 1985:

In the summer of 1982, it was announced that the Managing Director, Adrian Higham, was going to New York to take over

Charlie Stoll with his wife Lizanne, and Marjorie Redwood (left)

the entire International Division, previously ably headed by Marianne Orlando, on her retirement. This came as a complete surprise for a Brit to take up a major New York appointment, and a further surprise was in store when we heard that Charlie Stoll, a New Yorker, and a Vice President of Wiley Inc., would be acting MD for one year. This was a fortunate time for the UK office as Charlie, after Adrian's sterling work, got the operation nicely balanced, providing the solid foundation on which the last two successful years have been based.

Sadly Charlie Stoll died in 1994. John Collins, former General Manager of Jacaranda Wiley, wrote the following tribute to Charlie:

Remembering Charles B. Stoll, AB (Eng.), Scholar, Publisher and Gentleman

The Eng. stands for a Princeton degree in English. However the Marines believed it represented engineering and thus, inadvertently, laid the foundation for the development of one of Wiley's most humane and learned editors and publishers.

Charles Stoll was gifted and scholarly, but always, the dutiful servant of the house of Wiley for over 40 years as Regional Representative, Editor, Publisher, Corporate Secretary, Director and Vice President of the International Division. It was in this last role that he superintended the purchase of Jacaranda Press in 1976 and I then came to know him as boss, colleague and friend.

In no time everyone in the Australian connection came to respect the man for his generosity of spirit, his deep but broad-ranging abilities and understanding, his quiet but forceful patience; in a word, for his wisdom.

I came to admire him especially for his ability to handle all associates, whether they happened to be within the firm or outside, with the same quiet, almost undemonstrative, dignity. It was therefore natural that he should be held in such high regard by the Chinese, who also know how to marry perception with dignity. I often thought that Charlie had much in common with the Chinese intellectuals who suffered under the waves of misfortune known, perhaps euphemistically, as "cultural revolutions". In his own quietly patient way Charles Stoll weathered all the storms and change at Wiley to eventually become one of Wiley's most revered and trusted advisers.

He shared his humanity without fear or favour, and this more than anything else earned him respect in the worlds that I shared with him outside the US. As a negotiator he was both fair and firm, and he could be engagingly or annoyingly inscrutable when the occasion demanded it. There is something Bunyanesque in his pilgrim's progress through the sloughs of Wiley's publishing "reorganization". However, I prefer to salute the man, his works and his influence in Chaucerian terms:

"He was a verray, parfit, gentil knyght."

ETQ

Anyone who was at Wiley in the mid-1980s will remember the proliferation of "quality" programmes being marketed by management consultants in the USA and the UK. At Wiley we threw ourselves with great enthusiasm into one such programme—"Excellence Through Quality". However, not everyone was convinced by the promises of ETQ, and one sceptic was Keith Bowen, who joined Wiley as an accountant and subsequently became Distribution Manager when Roy Bottwood left in 1988. Keith left the company in 1992, but has sent us the following recollections about his experience of ETQ.

I NAME THIS SHIP ETQ: GOD BLESS HER, AND ALL WHO PAY TO SAIL IN HER

Keith Bowen (former Distribution Manager)

In the 1970s, an American (of course) by the name of Tom Peters was responsible for revolutionising company methodology for attempting to achieve their goals (or explaining to themselves why they were failing to achieve them) by the simple expedient of identifying a word which was to become a management training buzzword for many years, was to earn him a great deal of money, and was to enable many, many other self-appointed training gurus to board the bandwagon simply by using the same word—a word Peters must have been sick that he was unable to copyright. That word was, as if you need reminding, *"excellence"*.

Following his book, *In Pursuit of Excellence*, many other authors launched their version, aping the word and methodology, but giving their own local interpretation and making their version sufficiently different to avoid charges of plagiarism. One such was a jolly fellow named Mike Robson, author of *The Journey to Excellence*, which was to be published by Wiley in the UK. Such was the impact of his outpourings that it did not take the powers that be too long to realise that here was the man who could identify our shortcomings, put us on the right path to allow us to identify the reasons for the shortcomings and formulate ways of eliminating these shortcomings, with the end result that our customers would then be even more happy with the *excellence* of the *quality* of our product, spend more money with us, sell more of our books, make themselves rich, us rich, us popular, us up there with Marks & Spencer as icons of qualitative methods and product! *Wow*!

And so began a long period of self-examination. Anybody who was anybody, plus a lot more who just thought they were, became involved in audit teams in a variety of subjects, ranging from customer orientation, through examining how employees perceived each other, to company image, etc. Audit team facilitators were appointed and the audit teams launched themselves into a frenzy of questionnaire compilation, distribution, collection, analysis and giggling at the responses. I well recall that one particular team, who were investigating communication, discovered that the main way of finding out what really was going on in the company was to listen either to the man who ran the office cleaning company or to the painters. Even more startling was that one employee, who must remain nameless, had said that she found out all that she needed to know by pillow talk. No comment, but it was found to be true.

During the course of the programme, the company had a Christmas bash, and it was thought that this would be too good an opportunity to miss in terms of spreading the word and showing the very few who were not involved directly what was occurring. My abiding memory is of a member of one of the teams who had decided that the acronym ETQ did not have to stand for "Excellence through quality", and sat down for the entire weekend previous to the event with her partner, concocting other possibilities for the initials, and managed to cover what seemed in retrospect like a few lengths of wallcovering with the most appalling tripe. Examples: "entelechy through quiescence" (yes, we did challenge the word "entelechy", but she proved it does exist, although I have never found a dictionary since which lists it); "expedite through quintessentialism"; and my favourite, "elephants tolerate quinsy". As you might guess, this *really* grabbed the imagination of the non-cognoscenti, who were immediately possessed with a demonic urge to join an audit team by hook or by crook.

After a predetermined time, each audit team, who by now (in my case anyway) were thoroughly fed up with the words audit, team, excellence, quality, facilitator, customer, meeting, report, etc., prepared reports for presentation to the Board. These appeared to be well received, and we all sat back to await some Messianic diktat, some change in direction/objective/methodology/personnel/departmental organisation, or at the very least a pillar of fire.

I moved on about five years later, still waiting. I have frequently considered the number of hours which were consumed by ETQ, and wondered if a real and tangible benefit ever did accrue.

Well, actually, Keith, we can demonstrate quite a few tangible benefits, summarised by Mike Foyle in an article he wrote for *Grapevine* (the company newsletter then) in 1987.

ETQ

Mike Foyle (then Managing Director)

Much has been achieved in 18 months. Below is a list of what we've done. We have also just set up a Quality Council, which I shall personally chair, consisting of me, Mark Bide, Tim Davies, Peter Ferris, John Jarvis and John Wilde. We shall meet monthly to monitor all progress on training, quality circles, task forces, etc., and each director will be personally responsible for quality in his division.

There is no magic in ETQ: it depends on individuals committing to quality. Some of you perhaps expected a sort of miracle, and are critical or disappointed that no miracle has happened. But Mike Robson never promised us any miracles. He did promise to show a technique by which we could, little by little, step by step, begin to remove the defects from what we do, get things right first time, and meet our customers' needs.

Whether we call it ETQ or not, these things we must do, if the company is to survive and prosper.

Benefits to date
As a direct result of our first 18 months with ETQ, we have:

- a full-time staff training officer (Anne Scott)
- a company-wide training programme
- a new induction course
- job descriptions for all staff
- improved performance reviews
- a grading committee
- a team-briefing process for better communication
- a Wiley newsletter—*Grapevine*
- an active sports and social committee

Training
Our schedule of MRA courses is now complete for this fiscal year. Just in case you thought they were being left out, the directors will be attending two MRA courses: Running Meetings, and Dealing with People.

Around 120 people are taking part in other training courses ranging from fork-lift training to financial planning and cash flow

Mike Foyle with Brad and Esto Wiley, and Adrian Higham outside the Baffins Lane building

forecasting. We also have an ongoing PC training programme which is being co-ordinated by Tony Withers, our new PC Support Analyst.

Together with Mike Robson, we have started planning for F89 and would welcome your input on content, most suitable timing of courses, etc.

Other developments
Peter Ferris's Quality Task Force has tackled the long-standing problem of write-off, and has produced its report.

Teams will start work on business process management in May 1988. Among other things, they plan to look at ways of improving our internal publishing process and the ways and means of selling UK books in the US.

THE JAPANESE MARKET

Wiley's Tokyo office was established many years ago, and Hiroshi Tsukabe joined Wiley in 1968 as our representative for Japan and Korea. Responsibility for the Japanese market was transferred from Wiley New York to Wiley Chichester on 1st May 1989. At that time, Mike Foyle wrote:

Bob Long and Mike Foyle (back row) in 1989 presenting the Outstanding Performance Award to the Tokyo office team of Hiroshi Tsukabe (Manager); Yuko Yanaka (Customer Service Assistant); Tadashi Hase (Senior Representative); Setsuko Saito (Promotion Manager) and Taeko Nishikawa (Secretary)

Wiley regards the Japanese market as most important for our growth. It is a rich country with significant research in all areas of science, technology and medicine. Consequently we are increasing our marketing, promotion, sales and editorial efforts in this territory. The response of all the members of the Tokyo office has been tremendous. They have great increased the Wiley profile on all fronts—exhibitions, direct mail, advertising, bookseller support—and established excellent customer service links with Bognor Regis and Chichester. The end result has been a great increase in workload, but at all times they have been professional, efficient, very quick to respond to requests, and have exercised a high degree of quality assurance. As a result the Wiley Tokyo office won the Group Award for Outstanding Performance in 1989.

AN EVENTFUL YEAR

Mike Foyle summarised the company's achievements at the end of FY89 as follows:

> We can look back on another good year, with good sales, and profits above plan—a few soft spots here and there but overall a very satisfactory result.
>
> We are all getting used to the idea of living with change these days, and this year has been no exception. We have absorbed the Middle East as a sales territory, set up a new distribution arrangement in South Africa, and paid several visits to Japan in preparation for taking over, which happened in May; we have got all the New York journals onto our systems; we have streamlined and strengthened our publishing activities; further improved production processes and schedules; reorganised our marketing structure; taken on new lists for distribution; and weathered a postal strike. We have been asked to take on responsibility for Wiley's international information systems, and are in the process of installing new, more powerful IBM hardware.
>
> We have commissioned a major independent review of our jobs and salaries to make sure we are fully competitive, and have also kept up a considerable training programme. We have lost some people and have brought new blood in, and have adapted to changes in senior management in New York. An eventful year, in fact.

CHAPTER SIX

Editorial and Production

AN EDITOR REMEMBERS

Michael Coombs (Publisher, Psychology)

TO ACHIEVE better distribution in the UK and Europe and a base for editorial activity, Wiley Inc. set up Wiley Ltd in London in 1960. The acquisition of Interscience Publishers (a successful European-based high-level science publisher) added impetus to the editorial function. The first London editor was Ossian Goulding (previously editor with Interscience), with Ron Watson as Editorial Director.

The first Wiley Ltd publication in 1962 was *Advanced Inorganic Chemistry*, by Al Cotton at MIT and Geoffrey Wilkinson at Imperial College, London. This was co-published with Wiley Inc. and was an Interscience contract that came to Wiley with the acquisition. Interscience brought to Wiley a strong author base in Europe and it was to remain the imprint for Wiley's high-level science books for the next thirty years.

Who was there, and why?

Cotton and Wilkinson was a huge success. Wiley Inc. was one of the leading publishers at the senior college level in the US and was keen to establish a similar position as a textbook publisher in the UK and Europe, where post-war reconstruction had led to a major expansion of the universities and research centres. The Interscience link, however, brought us many opportunities for reference and journal publishing. In 1965 two more editors were appointed in London: Jamie Cameron (for reference books) and Mike Coombs (for textbooks). Ossian Goulding became Editorial Director, and handled the reference list in chemistry, as well as travelling extensively in Europe. The publishing programme was confined to the maths, science and engineering areas. When Wiley Ltd moved to

Chichester in 1967 the Editorial Department included three editorial secretaries, and with three editors published about 30–40 books a year!

Strange things called journals

Until the acquisition of Interscience and its small journal list, Wiley had no major interest or expertise in journal publishing. The worldwide post-war expansion of research and teaching in science and technology (particularly in the 1960s and 1970s) generated a huge market for reference books and journals. Wiley realised that journals were a Good Thing and Jamie Cameron and Ossian Goulding began to build up the Wiley journal list, starting now famous journals like *Numerical Methods in Engineering* and *Software Practice and Experience*. Later, Wiley bought another company, Heyden, whose list of established and growing journals established Wiley as a major journal publisher.

Thinking vertically

Journal publishing grew very comfortably alongside Wiley Ltd's reference publishing in that golden age of library expansion, and our high-level publishing became increasingly successful. It was high-margin, international business. In contrast, textbooks were lower margin and harder to sell internationally. In the UK, despite major expansion, student numbers were still small, professors were unaccustomed to "adopting" textbooks (or writing them!) and Europe was fragmented by language and educational systems. There were obvious tensions between the high-level and the text publishing, particularly when Wiley Inc. sought to become a major college publisher by seeking more low-level introductory and community college textbooks for the huge US markets.

In the early 1970s the Wiley Ltd editorial programme was reorganised along subject lines, into three sections: physical and engineering sciences (Jamie Cameron), Biological Sciences (a new editor, Mike Packard) and Social Sciences (a new programme, Mike Coombs). Each editor now published textbooks, reference books and journals. Vertical publishing had arrived!

By the late 1970s further subdivision of the subjects brought more specialist editors for chemistry (Dr Howard Jones) and biology (Dr Stephen Thornton), and the appointment of Jamie Cameron as

Editorial Director under a new Managing Director, Adrian Higham.

Sun, sand and bio-medicine

Adrian Higham came from Longmans, where he had considerable experience of school and language publishing for Commonwealth markets in Africa and the Far East. As the university markets were expanding in these tropical and developing countries, Wiley Ltd decided to launch a programme to serve their special needs. Mike Coombs was appointed editor for this new programme, with a mission to travel this world of sun, sand and poor plumbing, to acquire textbooks and reference books, and to seek out the best tropical beaches.

The largest Commonwealth market was Nigeria, where Wiley formed an alliance with Spectrum Books (a Nigerian company run by a Dutchman, Joop Berkhout) to market the Wiley list as a whole in Nigeria, and to collaborate with our efforts to publish for tropical and developing countries. Unfortunately, most of the African countries were slowly going broke, and the oil price collapse in the early 1980s accelerated this process in Nigeria. The tropical and developing countries programme ended in 1983.

Meanwhile, the growing importance of molecular biology, biochemistry and pharmacology had spurred Wiley Ltd to set up a new Biomedical Publishing Group under a new editor, a young

Mike Trimble (author), Celia Carden (editor) and Dorothy Rowe (author) at the 175 years of Wiley celebrations

Dr John Jarvis (who joined from Elsevier Publishers in Amsterdam to continue the development of the journal programme).

Modern times

The 1980s was a time of innovation. Wiley Ltd ventured into sponsored publishing (mainly for pharmaceutical companies) and a programme of nursing books. With John Jarvis now Editorial Director, the older publishing programmes were reorganised into Publishing Groups: Physical Sciences (under newly arrived Ernest Kirkwood), Maths and Engineering Sciences (under Ian McIntosh), Management and Computing (under Ian Shelley) and Psychology (under Mike Coombs), a small list which survived the sell-off of the Social Science lists in politics, sociology, architecture and geography, and which was eventually merged with the Management list. Also, for the first time, marketing assistants and executives were integrated into the Publishing Groups, to create knowledgeable and highly motivated teams.

The 1990s brought prominence at Wiley Inc. for the Professional and Trade book programme which had been quietly growing in the US market, and which now demanded international scope and attention. Law, accountancy and finance were now major Wiley interests.

In response to the growing importance of professional publishing, Wiley Ltd acquired the Chancery Law list in 1991, and in 1992 the Management and Psychology programme, together with the Chancery Law list, became the nucleus of a new Professional Publishing Division, initially headed by John Jarvis, and then in 1994 by Steven Mair.

In 30 years the Wiley Ltd publishing establishment has grown from one editor, then three (publishing 30 books a year), to a collection of Publishing Groups with dozens of editors, assistants, marketing executives and publishers, publishing about 400 books a year, and managing an expanding list of over 100 journals.

HOW JOURNALS GET STARTED

*The launch and life of IJNME
by O.C. Zienkiewicz (R.H. Gallagher)*

A journal can get started for a great variety of reasons. These range from a very common ambition of an individual to "have his own journal", or through a perceived need of a group seeking more specialized identification than that provided by existing publication outlets, and finally to that given by the emergence of a new research field. Numerical (or computational) analysis falls clearly in the last category and here is the reason for the start of the *International Journal of Numerical Methods in Engineering*, though inadequate representation of this field through established channels existed.

Finite difference methods and their solution by Southwell's relaxation methods provided the first focus of interest in the new subject during World War II when many real engineering problems required an urgent solution irrespective of the cost involved. It was here that the author of the present article started, soon finding, however, in his own academic career that the publication of articles was not easy. Many respected and well established journals on applied mechanics and mathematics refused publication on the general premise that numerical results were "one off", precluding general conclusions, while the background methodology itself was of little interest. The only possibility of publication remained that in engineering journals when a particular example of wide engineering interest was tackled and this could be used to guide further designs.

With the advent of the finite element method and the developments in digital computers which were a necessary precondition for it, the difficulties became even more pronounced. Not only was it possible now to obtain new solutions to problems of engineering and physics which were previously outside the range of possibilities, but new research concepts of mathematical or algorithmic methodology were expanding rapidly and demanding an outlet for publication. Further, such publications were urgently required by the engineering profession which was starting to use finite elements extensively.

The above needs became obvious to the author of this article who found that many of his colleagues in the field shared his views. In particular, a "young American"—Dick Gallagher—became very interested and after many discussions at various conferences during the period of 1965–1967 when our paths intersected, the idea of launching a new journal was hatched. Here we received much help from another friend. He was Ossian Goulding, the Engineering Editor of John Wiley & Sons in Chichester.

Ossian became acquainted with me through the publication of an edited volume dealing with the subject of stress analysis in 1965. This work was based on a conference/course run at Swansea University where an attempt was made to put together the latest developments in both numerical and experimental methods. The first (and only) printing of this book in 1964 produced 3,000 copies and these were sold within the first year after publication. Clearly, there was life in the subject and this book, with a series on Numerical Methods in Engineering which followed it, became our first common venture.

The publication know-how of Ossian meant that the "gestation period" of the journal was a short one and the decision to launch it on 1st January 1969 was taken. The year 1968 had therefore to be devoted to the preliminaries. However, the main problem, i.e. that of ensuring availability of papers, presented little difficulty. A few phone calls, letters and the "bush telegraph" (e-mail not being yet available) ensured sufficiency of papers for the first four issues within months.

The decision to publish the journal on a quarterly basis was taken initially but, in retrospect, we were fortunate that the words "Quarterly of ..." were not included in the title. Table 1 shows the rapid growth of the journal size and of the number of annual pages printed. Today 24 issues are printed each year, including nearly 5,000 pages of subject matter.

While on the subject of the title chosen, we discussed many alternatives at the time. The words "finite element" and "structural mechanics" were obviously much in our minds as at the time these were the main focus of interest. In retrospect I am glad that neither of these was incorporated. By avoiding them we allowed the journal to be fully "cross-disciplinary" and permitting interchange of information between various fields of application and various methodologies.

How was the journal received by the public and how well did it perform for the publisher? Well, it seems to me that the initial view of the "need" was well founded.

Table 1. *First 25 years of IJNME (1969–1993)*

Year	Volume	Issues	Total pages	No. of papers	No. of short notes
1969	1	4	401	25	—
1970	2	4	608	41	—
1971	3	4	601	41	6
1972	4/5	4 + 4	1209	94	16
1973	6/7	4 + 4	1206	82	50
1974	8	4	927	56	15
1975	9	4	959	53	13
1976	10	6	1428	88	34
1977	11	12	1920	110	45
1978	12/13	12 + 2(s)	2311	140	38
1979	14	12	1882	97	42
1980	15/16	12 + 1(s)	2062	116	37
1981	17	12	1892	105	21
1982	18	12	1888	106	26
1983	19	16	1886	112	14
1984	20	12	2333	142	18
1985	21	12	2310	145	(*)
1986	22/23	12 + 3(s)	3158	187	
1987	24	12	2432	139	
1988	25/26	12 + 2(s)	3443	198	
1989	27/28	12 + 3(s)	3613	205	
1990	29/30	8 + 8	3566	190	
1991	31/32	8 + 8	3542	173	
1992	33/34/35	10 + 10 + 3(s)	5385	279	
1993	36	24	4275	213	

(s) special topic issues
(*) "Communications journal" started

From the author's point of view we see from Table 1 that the publication rate, following of course the receipt of manuscripts and governed by it, continued throughout the 25 years of the journal's existence to rise rapidly. The high number of citations confirms that this was achieved while preserving the high quality.

From the publishers' (and the public's) viewpoint it appears from the start that the number of subscriptions was steadily increasing up to the last decade when the financial stringencies resulted in cancellations of subscriptions for most journals. I believe today the journal still holds the largest number of subscribers in the field which IJNME opened up. Indeed today a very large number of journals followed the lead. Some copied the "general style" of IJNME while others wished a more rapid access to specialized fields of application and limited the subject area.

Within John Wiley & Sons at Chichester a substantial number of such specialized journals exist today. It is with some pride that we recall being in a measure responsible for the birth of three of these; the *Journal of Structural Dynamics in Earthwork Engineering*, the *International Journal of Numerical Methods in Fluids*, and the *Journal of Analytical and Numerical Methods in Geomechanics*. In particular, the first of those whose editors were old friends Ray Clough and Geoff Warburton, was initiated at a special dinner in Liege, hosted by Ossian in 1971 when we were all present at IUTAM Conference on Computation in Elasticity. The name of the restaurant escapes my memory—it could have been Coq d'Or—it certainly was the best in town and Ossian performed as mine host leaving little to be desired.

In case some are given the impression that starting a journal is a path of roses all the way, I should add that there are many problems which have to be dealt with on a daily basis. The most common of these is the referee who lacks a sense of urgency and delays the reviews causing well understandable anger of the authors. Here editors have to pour oil on troubled waters.

More serious are problems of referee conflict and, fortunately rare, outbursts from outside the journal accusing authors—and also the editors—of publishing unworthy or plagiaristic material.

Publishers could well consider helping the editors of future journals by establishing sets of rules, or at least suggestions, on how to deal with such matters and passing these on to newcomers in the field, together with a computer program for management of the journal. Such computer programs today have to be recreated by all.

Computer network publishing is another matter as yet not fully solved but which again needs attention. However, all these are minor subjects compared with the feeling of achievements which publication of a successful journal brings. We have enjoyed and are enjoying both the work and the achievement.

PROFESSOR SAUL PATAI

Professor Saul Patai (Department of Organic Chemistry at the Hebrew University of Jerusalem) has been a Wiley author since

1964. He is editor of the renowned "Chemistry of Functional Groups" series, latterly joined by Professor Zvi Rappoport in 1994. The essence of the series was described in a modest 227-page book by Saul Patai entitled *Glossary of Organic Chemistry* and published by Wiley-Interscience in 1962. Since that time, 66 titles have been published in the series, but at the end of 1996 the actual number of books (bearing in mind that some were two-volume sets) including updates, reached a grand total of 98, consisting of 71,869 pages and written by 1,601 authors.

Above is a picture of Professor Patai standing next to the "tower" of his books, and Professor Rappoport next to those with which he was involved either as volume editor or series editor.

WHAT COLOUR WILL IT BE?

Heather Bewers (former Publishing Editor)

Heather Bewers, who left Wiley in 1990, was the Publishing Editor who worked on the series in the late 1980s. Heather wrote the following article in *Grapevine* in 1989 in celebration of Professor Patai's 25-year association with Wiley:

> If I had a fiver for every time I have been asked this, I would by now be considerably better off. Not being so lucky, it is a question I have come to dread. It signifies, for those not in the know, that the next Patai jacket is due, and the most critical factor, the colour, has to be selected. By now we have exhausted many of the possibilities, and my imagination is beginning to fail, to say nothing of the Pantone swatch. I quite clearly lack the tireless energy of Professor Saul Patai, for whom 1989 represents the 25th year of publishing with Wiley.
>
> The first volume was published in 1964, and has been succeeded by a further 42 volumes (in 62 parts) and comprising in all some 46,000 pages. I should add (hastily) that this is simply an interim report as there is no sign of the series (in organic chemistry) either declining or stopping and there are at least 12 volumes in the pipeline. In addition there is a recently initiated sub-series the Updates which looks like providing work for everyone for years to come.
>
> What these dry figures fail to show, and which is only partially visible in this photo of Saul Patai with his volumes is the immense vitality and charm of the series editor. Over 25 years, Saul has made and kept many friends at Wiley and few can have remained unaffected by some aspect of the series or its editor. Since he long ago acquired a long range information system, I am sure he will somehow see or hear of this "publication" so: Saul, congratulations and long may it continue. To all those involved with the series over the last 25 years, thank you for all your time and effort—but why have you left me with the choice of colours?

Rosie Altoft, then Publishing Editor for Computer Sciences, with authors at the opening of the Paris office in 1990

Gaynor Redvers-Mutton, Publishing Editor, (second on the left) with colleagues in the Tokyo office

PRODUCTION

Dennis Chaplin (former Production Manager)

It was quite by chance that I was given the opportunity to join the Production Department of John Wiley in 1970. At that time I was living in Guildford and working as Production Manager for IPC Science and Technology (later to become Butterworth Scientific), but wished to return "home" to Chichester. Whilst house hunting I called into Baffins Lane, to receive a "Don't ring us. We'll ring you" response to my enquiry regarding employment. However, they did ring me and, following an interview with Ron Watson (Managing Director) and Dennis Fairs (Production Manager), I was offered and accepted a position in the department.

In 1970 the Production Department was very small, in both staff and output. In addition to Dennis Fairs, there was Marjorie Redwood (Managing Editor) and a small number of copy-editors and production staff. All copy-editing and proof-reading was done in the department.

Some 35 new book titles were being produced each year, with a small number of reprints. As for journals, there were only four, all quarterly, each averaging 64 pages per issue. Compare that with now, with the 400 new books each year, the 200 reprinted titles, the 150 journals now producing 1,000 issues, and you are immediately aware of the incredible growth in output the department has achieved in 30 years. It is of interest to note that one of the original journals was *Numerical Methods in Engineering* (NME), which has increased from 256 pages in 1970 to 4,800 pages today. It was the success of *NME* and increased interest in the engineering community that paved the way for launching other titles in the numerical methods area—*International Journal of Numerical Methods in Fluids*, *Journal of Analytical and Numerical Methods in Geomechanics* and *Communications in Numerical Methods in Engineering*—which themselves now publish in excess of 5,000 pages each year. Two of our first book series titles were Patai's *Chemistry of Functional Groups* and Bajpai's *Advanced Mathematics*, both of which continued to be produced into the 1990s.

All but one of the staff from that time have now left the employment or retired. The sole survivor is Monica Twine, who joined just a few weeks before I did and who, in my opinion, should be contributing this piece. (Did you ever get to spend that weekend in

Market Rasen, Monica?) A very youthful-looking Martin Smart, Ian Jack and Irene Cooper were still to join us, and it was not until 1980 that our "poacher turned gamekeeper", Smyth Pollock, made the transition from Wiley Account Executive with Universities Press, Belfast, to Assistant Production Manager.

The department was first located on the west-facing side of the top floor of Baffins Lane. In the summer months it was unbearably hot, and on many occasions work in the Art Department was brought to a halt, because in a temperature of over 100° Fahrenheit it was impossible for the Indian ink to set on the line illustrations. By contrast, my office was in the centre of the building, without ventilation, heating or natural light, and was known by all as "the black hole of Calcutta". Happy memories. Compare this with the state-of-the-art Journals Production Department in Stocklund House!

Hot metal typesetting and letterpress printing was still the main method of book and journal production in the late 1960s/ early 1970s. Cold- and photo-composition with lithographic printing was in its infancy. Many of our first titles were produced by a combination of both; hot metal setting/reproduction pulls/ litho printing. All binding was sewn. Unsewn or "perfect" binding was just coming on to the scene and was far from "perfect". I can well remember standing in a very cold warehouse on the Terminus Road Industrial Estate examining 1,000 copies of one of our first "perfect" bound books and rejecting over 700 of them. Computer-assisted typesetting and author-generated/edited disks belonged to the far distant future, together with slotted or notched binding.

In 1975 the department was responsible for sending the first scientific manuscript to India for typesetting. It was one of Mike Coombs' behavioural sciences titles and it went to the Thomson Organisation in New Delhi. Thank you, Mike, for your confidence in us. "Informed" opinion was that we were mad and that it would all end in disaster, but there were no problems. It was very well typeset, the film was flawless and it was the forerunner of the many thousands of pages of complex mathematical typesetting produced each year in that country. It is pleasing also to note that our two companies continue to enjoy a close working relationship.

Later in the 1980s Dennis Fairs established the Text Processing Unit (later under the leadership of Geeti Granger) in order to process author-generated disks through to camera-ready copy. The department was once more in the forefront of a further development in production techniques.

A major landmark in the department's development came in 1987, with the appointment of Mark Bide as its first Production Director. Mark came to us from Holt-Saunders and quickly confirmed his reputation as a first-class production man. Prior to his appointment the department had always, apart from a short period, had a Publishing Editor as its director. It is regrettable, but true, that this led to a conflict of interests on occasions, with the result that working relationships between Editorial and Production were not always as smooth as they could have been. Under Mark's very firm and determined guidance, and with John Jarvis's support as Publishing Director, this was to change, and respect for each other's expertise and professionalism grew. Although Mark is no longer with the company it is my belief that his ideas, enthusiasm and influence still live on within the department. Because of this, and the skills and abilities of its current staff, the Production Department remains at the forefront of production techniques. It justifiably has the reputation of being among the top production departments in scientific publishing in this country. May it continue for the next 30 years and beyond.

INDEXING

Geoffrey Jones of Information Index, Gosport, Hants

My association with John Wiley began in the early 1970s when I was commissioned by Dennis Chaplin to compile an index. Many indexes and several staff members later, my company is still busy supplying indexes to John Wiley publications.

In the mean time there have, of course, been quite revolutionary changes in the process of publishing, and no less so in the world of indexing. Although, in general, a human brain is still necessary to generate index entries from the text, from that point onwards the process has largely been automated.

Perhaps the greatest contribution of technology to indexing has been in the process of alphabetical sorting. Originally this consisted of manually sorting separate cards or slips of paper, and a large index could take all day. With the latest hardware and software an average size book index can be sorted virtually instantaneously.

And, of course, this can be followed by similarly instantaneous transmission to the publisher by modern-day communications systems.

Wherever does the future lie, when we are already enjoying such technological wizardry? Certainly the publishing industry will not stand still; in the mean time many congratulations to both John Wiley and Chichester on achieving a 30-year partnership.

Wiley World published this article in the 1980s describing the arrival of the Apollo system.

WILEY LTD ADOPTS HIGH-TECH COMPOSITION

Cathy Pawlowski in Wiley World (NY)

John Wiley & Sons, Ltd in Chichester, England, has been making breakthroughs recently with the "Apollo project". While it may sound like an adventure in outer space, the project is actually an innovative computerized system for producing short, economical print runs of specialized publications.

Geeti Granger, Senior Manager, New Media Development, at EP96

Sally Kyte, Smyth Pollock, Dennis Chaplin and Monica Twine visit Dobbie Typesetting in November 1988.

Voted Sexiest Dressed Man at the 1991 London Book Fair – Graham Russel, Book Production Manager – being congratulated by Tuppy Owens, author of The Safe Sex Maniac's Bible

Journals Production Christmas lunch with Page Brothers in 1990. Pauline Maliphant, then Manager, made sure that everyone took off the Galliard Printers sweatshirts before Page Brothers arrived! In 1996 all except three of the people pictured were still at Wiley. Back row: not known, Andrew Thrasher, Debbie Harris, Tim Scott, Janine Toole, Alison Archer, Jo Taylor, Simon Newton. Front row: Brian Southward, Martin Smart, Pauline Maliphant, Melanie Peet, Suzanne Richardson.

Short print runs cost more per copy than long print runs because the costs are the same to make printing plates and set up a press. And since many of Wiley's products have small, targeted audiences, their print runs are often very short and expensive.

Most academic monographs fall into this category. According to Peter Ferris, technical development manager for Wiley Ltd, "Publishers were printing more books than they could sell. 1500 copies of a monograph were being printed and only 800 were being sold. Five or six years ago, nobody ever worried about writing off unsold stock—now it is everybody's concern."

Last year, when Ferris proposed an investment in computerized systems, his first priority became the economic printing of short-run technical publications. The magic print run seems to be about 500 copies. Below that number, traditional publishing techniques are hopelessly uneconomic—above that number, there are opportunities for economies of scale.

The entire Wiley system comprises the Apollo workstation equipped with a 70 megabyte hard disk, QMX Laser-grafix 1200 printer, a magnetic tape unit, Tex software and a Mitsui optical character scanner that the company is using to feed text directly from the typed pages of an author's manuscript into the system. The Apollo system can also interface with manuscripts on floppy disk and tape.

The first volume to be produced on the system—a 200-page dictionary of medical acronyms—is already in the printing stage. The system isn't being used to actually print copies of books; rather it uses the system to produce either a single, high-quality original from which printing plates can be made or a magnetic tape which a printer can use to drive a phototypesetter or high-speed laser printer.

Publishing costs can be cut by up to 40% using these methods, according to Ferris. He also pointed out that the system can open new short-run publishing opportunities for Wiley in such areas as newsletters and journals.

The next step is to add a graphics camera that can digitize line drawings and enable finished pages to be produced on a laser printer. The long-term goals of this system are to reduce investment in inventory, reduce overall publishing risk, and better meet the market needs of the future.

CHAPTER SEVEN

Servicing Our Customers

CUSTOMER SERVICE

Karin Davies (Customer Service Manager)

IN 1967 Customer Service, as we know it today, was handled by four departments. Orders were received and "sorted" by Sales. It was here that most telephone calls were handled.

Order Processing consisted of:

Order Editing—highlighting author/short title with the help of the trade catalogue, which had to be manually updated. The Order Editing Clerk was in charge of the telephone.

Order Coding—Irene Merry recalls there was a long table in the middle of the office, on which were trays containing ready-to-use punch cards. First you found a card with your customer's account number. Following this was the ISBN card (in units of 1, 5 and 10). Naturally, when you needed a specific punch card the tray was empty, which meant asking the Computer Department to produce more cards before you could carry on. Having assembled your pile of cards, you would be lucky enough to have someone knock your little pile over! The job was tiring and monotonous.

Then, as now, Wiley was always ready to use new technology when if offered positive benefits, so in mid-1968 we replaced the long table with tubs, some containing customer and others title details. Orders were handwritten onto coding sheets and passed to punch card operators for keying.

Punchcard Operation/Verification—This really was state-of-the-art technology. Little red lights flashed every time the verifier found an error on a punch card. Wasn't it exciting?

Computer Input/Output Control—The punch card batches, manually added and recorded on a control sheet, were edited. "Error" and "wrecked" cards (the computer's favourite pastime was mangling as many punch cards as possible) had to be corrected. It was in this area also that the sales and returns totals were recorded in *the* control

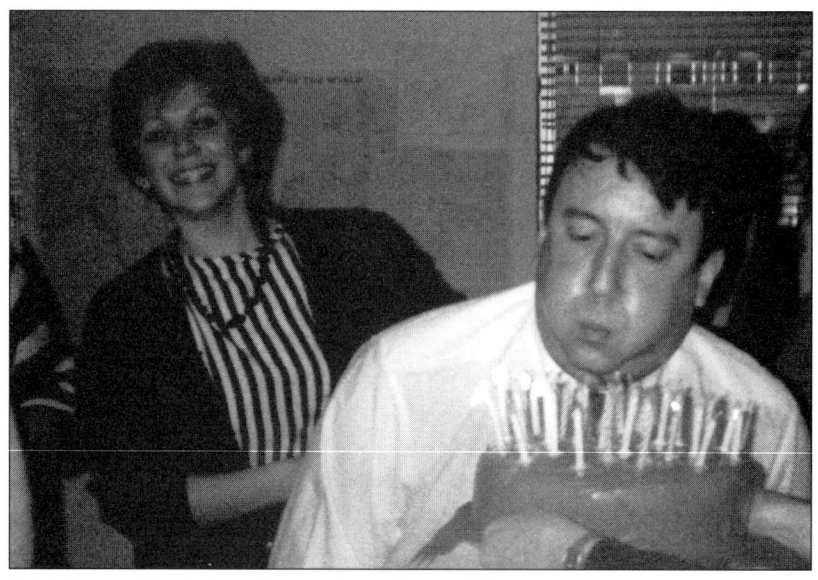

Keith Bowen, Distribution Manager from 1988 to 1992

book, with the help of an adding machine that had the capacity to add up to £99,999 19s 11d. This worked fine until 1970, when sales totalled over £100,000. It was then that a "modern" calculator appeared on the scene. Yet more new technology for the department!

Invoices were checked before being sent to our warehouse subcontractors.

Kirk Encyclopedia invoices, billed and checked by us in the UK, were shipped to the USA, where the books were dispatched.

Claims/credits, cash sales and proformas reported to our Accounts Department.

Dates we remember 1970–1982

1970 Opera 70 was formed. Several Wiley people were on the committee. The first opera, La Bohème, was staged at the Esplanade theatre in Bognor. Who were the "shoppers" in Paris? Most of our department. We did feel important.
Sales figures passed the £100,000 mark.
It was round about this time that Wiley had their first carnival float. Where was it built? In the Order Processing office. (It was a large "wise" owl.)

1973 Electricity restrictions due to oil cuts. Our Coding Clerks soldiered on by candlelight.
Who stole, two days before Mother's Day, the large rubber

Karin Davies, Customer Service Operations Manager, celebrating 20 years at Wiley—sealed with a kiss from Peter Ferris

plant from outside our office, just by the front door? And who stole that complete roll of green carpet, the first in our office? Own up now!

1974 Production of first computerised *full* title printout.
Our first VDUs!

1975 Order Processing took over Claims and Credit Checking. The department title became Customer Service.

During the years up to the move to Bognor strangers regularly wandered into the office looking for tax inspectors. We found this hard to understand as, in our experience, most people try to avoid them where possible.

People called asking for prices of the plants we had on our window sills. Even the local paper reported that it was worth walking past Baffins Lane to see the wonderfully decorated Wiley windows.

The guys in the Post Room used to invite us to taste their home-made wines—usually excellent, but some would have made very effective rocket fuel.

1977 In December we moved to Bognor. Because we felt so sad we were given permission to purchase Christmas decorations, at the company's expense. We put these up the day before we moved, only to find that the building was so damp that most of them had fallen down when we arrived the next morning. Two days before we moved, we nearly went on strike because

Celebrating coming 8th in the Booksellers Association survey in 1983, Roger Faulkner, Margaret Green, Sally Wade and Karin Davis

there was no bannister rail alongside our stairs. Our protest resulted in some rapid action by the builders.

We now had plenty of telephones and on-line VDU facilities to process our orders. Luxury!

1982 Fax installed. We received at least two a week!

In the warehouse, where our overflow filing was kept, we reached the stage of storing either books or filing. We invested in in-house microfilm facilities.

While at Bognor, we organised some great parties (Hallowe'en, fancy dress, Easter bonnet competitions and others). The first Wiley treasure hunts were organised by Customer Service.

Lynne Barc as the Mad Hatter and Sarah Morris as a schoolgirl

Sarah Morris and Mark Dodge

1989 Comic Relief Day—*(a) Geri Rogers is arrested by Peggy Bradley (b) Deanna Waldron and Peggy Bradley (c) Titus Olbrich and Gwenda Keates*

JULIE PEARSON

When Journals Manager Julie Pearson left the company in 1989, Mike Foyle described her as someone who had "grown up with the company over 20 years". Julie, he said, had contributed greatly to building Chichester's excellent reputation for journal fulfilment.

Margaret Radbourne joined the company, as Journal Administration Manager in 1990. Mark Bide, then Production and Distribution Director, wrote the following article in *Grapevine*.

Journals Admin, Christmas 1984—Liz Birtle, Carol Grainger, Sheila Woodrow, Iris Bull, Julie Pearson, Lyn Udall

WELCOME MARGARET

Mark Bide (former Production and Distribution Director)

Margaret Radbourne joined us at the beginning of January as Journal Administration Manager, from B.H. Blackwell Ltd, where she was Operations and Publishing Services Manager for their Periodicals Department, a subscription agent. Margaret had worked for Blackwells since she left school (a few years ago is all she will admit to).

She has lived in or around Oxford all her life, and has two teenage daughters. Her husband works in the transport industry. Since she is currently doing a 100-mile each way commute (when not staying in the company flat in Chichester), she says she has little time for any outside interests at the moment (although she says she is an expert darts and bar billiards player, which may tell you something about one of her occasional activities . . .).

Margaret has joined us at an extremely important time for the Journals Administration Department. Following the takeover by Chichester of responsibility for fulfilment of Wiley New York journals in 1988, last year we took on the Liss journals as well: the department is now handling more than three times the number of subscriptions it had two years ago. The volume of work has meant that we are a bit behind in processing orders for 1990 subscriptions, but thanks to very hard work (and some very long hours) from the department, the backlog is being cleared.

Only five weeks after joining Wiley, Margaret was on her way to New York, to meet her internal customers at Wiley and Liss. Margaret is no stranger to the US, having travelled there frequently for Blackwells; she already knew a number of Wiley people before joining the company.

Her experience as a journal subscription agent (about 80% of our journal subscriptions are handled through agents) will be of great value to Wiley in building our expertise in this key part of our business. We wish Margaret well in her new career in publishing.

Clive Newman

JOURNALS ADMINISTRATION DEPARTMENT

Carol Grainger and Helen Taylor who between them have worked for Wiley for 37 years

As you will see from the following, the Journals Department has grown somewhat in the past 23 years.

In 1974 there were four staff who looked after four journals, which we are still publishing today. Wiley was also the sole United Kingdom agent for a company in Switzerland which published mainly medical journals.

You might think this was probably a bit of a doddle; one journal for each member of staff. It wasn't. Everything was processed manually. Each invoice typed was an individual process until 1977, when continuation stationery was introduced. The typing of renewal invoices took from September to March. This was no easy task, as there were five copies, and if there was a mistake, as they were being sent to subscribers, it had to be retyped.

Once the invoices were typed, the details had to be written on the subscribers' index cards, which were filed and kept in the office. When payment was received, the information had to be marked on the subscriber's card and on copies of the invoice, one of which was then sent to the Accounts Department to update their records. Then labels had to be typed so that the journal issues could be sent to the customer.

Labels were kept in the department until the relevant issue(s) were published. Stock of journal issues was kept in a room Wiley had in an office in North Pallant. The Journals Clerks, as they were called then, two or three times a week at the end of the day, took envelopes and labels to North Pallant and boxed up the required number of issues to be despatched. They also, on a regular basis, had to count the number of copies still in stock for each issue in case a reprint had to be made.

All this work was carried out in two rooms on the first floor of Baffins Lane. In 1977, when Customer Service moved to Bognor, Journals moved to the ground floor in Baffins Lane.

1980(ish) saw partial computerisation. Haven't we progressed?

BOOK INFORMATION DEPARTMENT

Wendie Westwood and Peggy Bradley, who between them have worked for Wiley for 46 years

The Book Information Department was better known to us "old ones" as Bibliography and was managed under the careful and methodical eye of T.A.N. Henderson. Although the name and management were changed we considered that the work of publishing books was still carried out to the high standards that we had always worked to.

The computer age didn't really affect Book Information. We still had to manually update enormous record cards called "history cards" which were kept neatly in alphabetical order and by agency name. God help us if one went missing! The history cards were kept in metal trays until we ran out of space, when these were replaced by huge round metal towers which spun round for easy access.

To prepare for publication we had to manually stamp the date

When things get too hot ... Customer Service staff Jacque Allen, Matthew Collins, Sarah Mason, Jenny James, Thelma Watson and Stuart Taylor in 1994

Di Butterly and Margaret Jackson showing a leg at the 25-year anniversary celebrations

on each card and photocopy the computer details, which were then passed to the Computer Department, where they transferred the information onto a punch card. We didn't have a computer in those days to produce the nice publication sheet that you receive today, but instead a poor-quality stencil which was typed and placed onto a duplicating machine, which took forever!

So did the processing of continuation orders, i.e. customers who required the next volume published in any series. Again, we had huge cards and each time a volume was published we had to stamp the ISBN onto these, photocopy them and send them for processing to the Customer Service Department. Later these photocopies were returned to us, we then extracted the invoice number and date, and placed this information onto our cards in case of a customer enquiry. We didn't need to go to a multi-gym: with all the pen pushing, stamping, lifting and filing, we had all the exercise we needed.

We were then moved to Bognor Regis, where life wasn't quite the same, and by now most of our work was computerised. The main difference now is that books are published daily instead of weekly.

A Wiley donation to Bognor Regis library. Janet Hill (far right) joins the fun.

CHANGES IN BOGNOR

Mike Ridge joined the company in 1992. *Grapevine* published the following announcement:

> Mike Ridge is running a tight ship down at Bognor (his background is airforce, despite the maritime terminology). He has taken on the position of Distribution Manager and reports to Jim Dicks and is making sure that Wiley keeps up with the very best in the distribution league. All the stock is jumping to order...

In 1995 Margaret Radbourne (General Manager, Journals Admin/Customer Service) reported in *Wiley Europe* the following update on a major transatlantic initiative—the new journals fulfilment system.

> *After two years of intensive effort by the US/UK teams the new journals fulfilment system is up and running*
>
> Phase A of the new system, which has taken 2½ years to develop, was successfully implemented on 26th September. The system was developed jointly by both Wiley Inc. and Wiley Europe management teams and all programming was carried out in Chichester utilising virtually all our IT resources. To some this may have been frustrating as other projects had to go on hold. Was it worthwhile? The answer, I believe, is an unqualified yes!
>
> Phase A actually gave 53 quantifiable advantages over the old system, too many to list here. Its main benefit will be the flexibility it offers in enabling marketing and editorial teams to grow our journal business more efficiently.
>
> *Key features are:*
>
> - flexible discount, pricing and renewal structures
> - ability to sell multiple journal packages (with or without supplements, CD, videos etc)
> - ability to sell multi-year and multi-title packages

- ability to handle non-calendar annual subscriptions
- highly detailed on-line sales reporting
- greatly improved reporting of financial performance

Phase B has already begun and will enable us to handle rolling journals (those where subscriptions can start at any time during the year) and will allow more flexible subscription models for our calendar year journals. Electronic Data Interchange (EDI) will be one of the main thrusts allowing us to communicate with our trading partners electronically for the purpose of sending the agents price list, despatch information, and receiving and responding to claims. For marketing there will be better reporting and analysis of direct mailing campaigns, and the facility to produce system-generated letters to send with renewals, sample copies and follow-ups. We'll bring you news of progress with Phase B enhancements in due course—but its main purpose is to provide the final system capabilities for what will be the smartest fulfilment system in our industry.

CHAPTER EIGHT

The 1990s

THE FOLLOWING are a collection of items (some written at the time) reporting significant events in the 1990s.

In January 1990 Mike Foyle recalled the events and achievements of the 1980s.

A NEW DECADE

We have passed through a decade during which we have created considerable growth, especially in our own publishing, and particularly in journals. Growth has been evident everywhere: in editorial and production, marketing and distribution, in accounts, DP, and support activities; sales have more than tripled and profits grown five times.

And yet anything that has happened to this company in the last 10 years dwindles into insignificance in the perspective of the astonishing events which unfolded in Eastern Europe during 1989.

Perhaps it is not entirely fanciful to believe that Wiley has had some part in them. Wiley's publications, especially our books, have been imported into all those countries in numbers as great as, probably greater than, those of any other Western publisher. Our marketing people, our editors and our authors have visited those countries regularly, and maintained continuous contact with many of their citizens.

Science and technology progress by the objective observation of phenomena, by imaginative effort, by experiment repeated in many parts of the world, by the testing of hypotheses against established fact—in short by the never-ending effort to reject falsehood and establish the truth.

Our authors and contributors are all trained in this tradition whatever country they come from and their thoughts and ideas go into the books and journals we publish for them. There is no doubt in my mind that these people and these ideas have contributed to what we saw in East Europe last year.

GOODBYE TIM

Early in the new decade, Mike Foyle announced the departure of Tim Davies who had been our Finance Director for five years. Tim's unrivalled energy and commitment had greatly influenced the way we approached many aspects of our business. *Grapevine* reported on Tim's departure.

> More than 100 people gathered to bid farewell to Tim Davies at a party held on 16th February in the Chichester District Council Offices.
>
> Tim has left Wiley to work as International Finance Director at Pergamon Press in Oxford. Mike Foyle, who had returned from New York especially for the occasion, presented him with a cut-glass decanter and bottle of vintage port bought from a collection made throughout the company. He thanked Tim for all his work, recalling his arrival in the company seven years ago when in city suits and brightly coloured braces he came to "put a rocket under us all".
>
> In his speech, Tim thanked his own department staff for their dedication, and acknowledged the work and help from all the others. He recounted some amusing tales of trips to Nigeria, made with Keith Bowen, when their living conditions were far from "five star".
>
> Peter Ferris also said a few words of thanks and hastily explained that his jeans and jumper attire was due to him having come hot-foot from stock-taking at the warehouse.
>
> Also present to wish Tim well were retired directors Harry Newman and Jim Durrant.
>
> A magnificent cake portraying a memo, calculator and figure work had been specially commissioned, as had his caricature goodbye card.

MIKE FOYLE'S ROUND-UP OF THE FINANCIAL YEAR MAY 1989 TO APRIL 1990

We have had another excellent year, beating our profit target comfortably and getting 10% profits out of our book programme—despite continuing difficulties in the market, and an unprecedented amount of internal change.

Just consider some of the things that have happened since May last year:

- Half of the Chichester people moved offices, some more than once;
- We took on the fulfilment of Liss journals at short notice, and acquired a new journals administration manager;
- We divested the Media Medica business;
- We bought six Heyden journals;
- We got rid of many agencies and took on new distribution lists;
- We took over responsibility for Japan;
- We restructured marketing;
- We shortened our book and journal production cycle further;
- We hosted a visit by the New York Board;
- In DP, we created the Core System, and installed two new computers;
- We tidied up our personnel practices, introduced better appraisals and objective-setting, and long-service awards;
- We started an R&D group, and got other task forces working on book cover design, management information, marketing, manuscript submission, author support, our image in the community, telecommunications, and others.

To have achieved our results while all these things were going on is a fine record; we can rightly be proud of it; I congratulate you and thank you all sincerely.

MARK BIDE'S GLOBAL ASSIGNMENT

In the spring of 1991, Mark Bide, Production Director for Wiley Chichester, was appointed to the new position of Director, International Publishing Technology and Services. In that role, he focused on strategic issues concerning the production, manufacturing and inventory management of Wiley products worldwide,

The Board of Directors in 1991: Mark Bide (Production), Peter Ferris (Systems and Distribution), Jim Dicks (Finance), Mike Foyle (MD), John Jarvis (Publishing)

both books and journals, where real value could be added, costs reduced and competitive position improved.

According to Charles Ellis, the new position was created because "we believe strongly that there are opportunities for Wiley to benefit from a more global approach to production, manufacturing and inventory control."

Mark, who retained his responsibilities as production director in addition to his new position, examined many topics, including the electronic delivery of information and the establishment of worldwide relationships with suppliers. "I am here to raise questions," he said at the time. "This is just a first step in learning to serve what has become a global marketplace."

NEW FINANCE DIRECTOR

The following announcement of Jim Dicks's appointment appeared in *Grapevine* in March 1991:

Welcome to Jim Dicks, who has just joined as Finance Director. Jim used to work for Unwin Hyman Ltd in London, part of the Rupert Murdoch News Corporation Group.

Jim trained as a chartered accountant with Coopers and Lybrand in his home town of Northampton, and gained experience with several companies before moving into publishing in 1988. Married with two children, Jim plans to move to the Chichester area from Berkshire in the near future. I am sure everyone wishes him success in his new appointment.

SOVIET JOINT VENTURE

A joint venture was established in Moscow, with Nauka, the publisher of the Soviet Academy of Sciences in the early 1990s.

It was to explore the potential within the Soviet domestic market and for translating Russian scientific publications into English for worldwide distribution. A better partner could not have been found—since Nauka were the largest scientific publisher in the Soviet Union.

We provided computer software and hardware and Nauka provided office space and editorial, sales and support personnel.

Although several projects came to fruition, it was a great disappointment to us when the relationship was no longer tenable in the difficult and confusing times following the break up of the Soviet Union.

A little later, back in the UK, we were entering a new publishing area for Chichester:

WILEY ACQUIRES CHANCERY LAW PUBLISHING

In April Wiley purchased Chancery Law Publishing Ltd, a London legal publisher, from Bloomsbury Publishing Ltd. The acquisition was made through Wiley's European company, based in Chichester, UK.

Chancery was founded in 1989 by Andrew Prideaux and Jane Belford, former Managing Director and Publishing Director at Sweet & Maxwell, with the support of Bloomsbury, Its list comprises journals, books and updateable looseleaf manuals providing specialist information and services focusing on European Community law and selected areas of commercial practice for the legal and professional market.

"This acquisition helps us to begin realizing a long held strategic objective to enter European-based legal publishing as a complement to Wiley's subscription-based US law line," said Michael Foyle, Managing Director of Wiley UK. "It creates the foundation for a new international law publishing force."

Nigel Newton, Managing Director of Bloomsbury, added, "The strength of the Chancery list is a tribute to the long-term vision of Andrew Prideaux and Jane Belford who perceived the potential of European law publishing."

"The combination of the recent successful launch of the European Practice Library and the international strength of ownership by Wiley ensures a dynamic new phase in the growth of Chancery Law Publishing Ltd," said Andrew Prideaux.

from *Wiley World* 1992

Ian McIntosh who left Wiley in 1996, pictured here with John Jarvis

BONJOUR, STRASBOURG!

For some time, we have been committed to increasing our editorial presence in continental Europe. Since many of our books and journals have European authorship, the unification of Europe this year is likely to increase the importance of scientific, technical and medical publications originated there. We have, therefore, established an office in Strasbourg, geographically located in the centre of Western Europe.

The office is headed by Ian McIntosh, who continues as Publisher of the Technology Group. We anticipate special editorial benefits in the technology area, since France and Germany are major players in fields such as telecommunications.

from *Wiley World* 1992

Mike Coombs, John Jarvis and Mike Foyle in the reception area of the Strasbourg office

A NEW MANAGING DIRECTOR IN CHICHESTER

1992 continues to be a significant year. Not only is it the twenty-fifth year that John Wiley & Sons Ltd has been in Chichester but the appointment of the fifth managing director to serve in Chichester has been announced by Mike Foyle.

John Jarvis, Publishing Director of John Wiley and Sons Ltd, became Deputy Managing Director on 1st July 1992 and will take over as Managing Director from 1st May 1993. Dr Jarvis says of his appointment "Michael Foyle will be a difficult act to follow, but he has bequeathed me an exceptionally strong team of people. I intend to maintain and develop our record of high profitability while nurturing our culture of openness and enjoyment, which has made Wiley one of the most sought-after places to work."

John Jarvis holds a PhD from the University of Wales and spent 5 years in cancer research and teaching in cell biology at Cardiff and Bristol Universities, before entering publishing with Elsevier in 1977. He has been with Wiley since 1979 and set up and managed the Chichester biomedical publishing programme. He later became Editorial Director and then Publishing Director in 1989.

from *Grapevine* 1992

WILEY OPENS OFFICE IN LOUVRES

Wiley Europe s.a.r.l., a new division formed to enhance the development of European business, has registered offices near Paris in Louvres, France.

Wiley has had a strong sales presence in Europe for more than 30 years, with permanent representatives in Paris, Amsterdam, Oslo, Stuttgart and Madrid. The Strasbourg office was opened in 1991, and REDEL s.a.r.l. (a Professional Language Training Program relaunched as Wiley PLT) was purchased in 1992. Wiley PLT will now operate from the Louvres office, publishing English-language training materials for professionals. Wiley-Interscience-Europe will operate out of the Strasbourg office. The Strasbourg and Louvres offices will form the two trading branches of Wiley Europe s.a.r.l.

> John Jarvis, Managing Director of Wiley Europe, stated that "Wiley's UK base has provided a strong and successful presence for the company in Europe, but we recognize the importance of greater integration with our continental partners. These initiatives will help bring our marketing and sales operations closer to their customers, and our editors closer to their authors."
>
> <div align="right">from <i>Wiley World</i> 1992</div>

Annick Heitz and Bob Long

Jan de Landtsheer, Strasbourg's editor

Steven Mair, Director of the Professional Division, pictured on the right, with John Jarvis and John Heptonstall

WILEY IN PROFESSIONAL MARKETS

Sarah Stevens (Professional Publishing Director)

The need to expand Wiley's professional publishing programmes became starkly clear in the early 1990s. The predicted "doomsday" effect of electronic media on STM journals, the emergence of most of Europe from recession rekindling the market for high quality, business-orineted information, and the successful culmination of the European Union's 1992 programme set the scene.

Wiley responded in dynamic fashion to the changing environment and, by 1994, the Professional Division was born—a strategic step toward expanding and organising our publishing to match these new demands.

Chancery Law Publishing, a small law publisher based in London and specialising in European law, was acquired; Richard Baggaley was hired to build an indigenous list in finance and economics; the management programme had already tasted success with cutting-edge topics like business process reengineering, and we refocused our psychology programme into the growing areas of clinical psychology, criminal and forensic psychology, and child protection and welfare. Aided by high-profile books from our US colleagues, we rapidly established ourselves in the marketplace as a serious player.

Bringing together our various professional publishing programmes into a single division was fomalised with the appointment of Steven Mair in August 1994 as Publishing Director for the Professional Division and symbolised our intention to build a £7.5 million operation in 5 years.

Coming to the end of FY98 we are poised to deliver in excess of £10 million. The division continues to grow and prosper—we have added the Architecture, Earth and Environmental Sciences group, which, along with Law and Finance, will move to our offices in London in July 1997. This presence will allow all elements of the Professional Division to stay close to our author base, and to be an increasingly painful thorn in the sides of our competitors.

And meanwhile we continue to increase our presence in the city.

HELLO! TO WEST STREET

Claire Plimmer (Publishing Editor)

Glamorous offices seek fun-time tenants. These were the words that John and Jim read in the *Observer* with fervid excitement. Months of undercover negotiation are over and it's all out of the closet now, so here is a professional woman's view:

For those of you who equated a trip from Baffins Lane to Rowan House with a Channel crossing, the journey to West Street will seem like a transatlantic flight (economy class). Company compasses will be made available to assist those, like the post room, who didn't even discover the route to Rowan House. Easily accessible from the main drag, West Street will make a handy stop-off towards the end of lunch hour. And, for those unable to meet the challenge of such a daunting expedition, a carrier pigeon service (for messages not people) will be in operation.

Our modest new tenement enjoys the proximity to the Cathedral, A&N's china department and the armoury shop

> down the road. Unfortunately Saddlers, Woodies and the like are a bit of a hike from there but visitors will be welcomed with tea and coffee. For special treats we will be making an arrangement with the Bishops' Palace Tea Room—orders in advance for savoury mince.
>
> Just remember, before attempting the journey, bring your passport, or collect one from the Post Office. We look forward to seeing you down there.
>
> from Grapevine 1994

In May 1996, after many years of attempts to gain a significant publishing foothold on the Continent, we were successful in a highly competitive situation in acquiring one of the major STM publishers, VCH Publishers.

Originally established as the publisher of the German Chemical Society, VCH had become a major commercial publisher in its own right.

> ## VCH
>
> ### *Bob Long (Sales and Marketing Director)*
>
> At 2.25 am on the morning of 7th May 1996, Tim King put his signature to the contracts which secured the acquisition of VCH Verlagsgesellschaft and Wiley achieved a major strategic breakthrough. First, we became the world's largest publisher of primary journals in chemistry and the world's second largest journals publisher. At the same time we became one of the largest publishers in Germany and a major force across the whole of Europe, and we formed a major European alliance with the German Chemical Society. All in all, not a bad night's work. For those of us who were there it marked the end of a highly intensive week where breakfast became almost the meal of the day, sleep was something other people did, and the team simply worked on and on to get the job done. There were plenty of lows and highs as we made gradual progress but any over-enthusiasm was checked by an alternately stern, tetchy, fatigued or humorous invocation by someone that "it ain't over till the fat lady sings". At 4 a.m. that morning, as the champagne glasses crashed together,

Peter Clifford, New York Office's Vice President, Finance; Tim King, Vice President, Planning & Development and Jim Dicks

you can imagine the thumping enthusiasm of our toast—"the fat lady has finally sung".

The deal was done in the space of seven days in Frankfurt due to our simultaneous contractual, due diligence and negotiation work, something usually done over an extended period, the bulk of the strain being borne by Peter Clifford, John Jarvis, Tim King (above all others) and Dick Rudick. Jim Dicks, Ernest Kirkwood and I were there ploughing through the due diligence. Nothing of what was achieved would have been possible without our advisors, especially our indefatigable lawyer Klaus Stephan, and our investment banker Werner Pfaffenberger of JP Morgan, who were both tireless professionals of the very first rank. But just as importantly the deal would not have been done without the work in the preceding six months by the Vanadium Acquisition Team and colleagues in Chichester and New York, all too numerous to mention here but who all deserve grateful thanks. So overall, we succeeded because we raised our game to create a unique piece of international teamwork and energy to carry the day. We will need more of the same from all of us as we welcome our new VCH colleagues into Wiley and together develop our ideas for building a superb international business. I enjoyed every minute in Frankfurt, but the best is yet to come.

from *Wiley Europe*

WILEY WINS PUBLISHER OF THE YEAR—AGAIN

Trevor Armstrong (UK Sales Manager)
Stefan Usansky (National Accounts Manager)

The Wiley delegation arrived at the 26th annual CUBG (College and University Booksellers Group) conference in Malvern in March 1997, hopeful of repeating last year's success in winning the Publisher of the Year award. You will recall that in 1996 Wiley won five of the eight categories.

The results this year were even more stunning—we won seven categories! The only classification we failed to win was "terms" and even here we came second. At least Jim Dicks will be pleased.

Thirty-three publishers' performance throughout the last year was judged by sixty-seven booksellers and the final results showed that Wiley scored an average of over 80%, almost 0.5% higher than our nearest competitor.

We repeated our first-place positions in Marketing, Head Office Support, Bibliographic Information, Returns and Packing, and this year we won the Invoicing and Delivery Times for the first time. We also significantly improved our "Hotline" performance to appear in third position. The meeting chairman proclaimed Wiley as the "publishing benchmark" in these areas of service to the book trade.

We can all feel justly proud of this achievement which reflects the high level of service we give to our customers and although just a few of us collected the award it was on behalf of everyone who works in Chichester and Bognor. Well done.

CHAPTER NINE

Special Occasions

100 PRINTERS COME TO SAY GOODBYE TO DENNIS

Mark Bide (former Production Director), October 1990

WE REACHED the end of an era on 8th June, when Dennis Chaplin retired from Wiley just a few months short of his twentieth anniversary with the Company. As all of you who had the opportunity to work with him will know, Dennis was a very dedicated and hard working manager; we will miss him.

We could not allow this occasion to go unmarked; indeed Dennis had been planning it for some time. He wanted an opportunity to say goodbye not only to his friends from Wiley past and present, but also his many friends in the printing industry. We set aside his last three days to buffet lunches: the first two for suppliers and the final one, on the actual day of his retirement, for Wiley and ex-Wiley employees.

It says a great deal for the way in which Dennis has won the friendship and respect of those he has worked with over the years that well over 100 representatives of the printing industry came to Chichester over two days to mark his retirement. The photograph shows one of those gatherings, in Stocklund House. Guests came from far and wide. The furthest anyone came was from Delhi (although in honesty it must be said that they were in London already); however, a significant contingent flew from Belfast for the day for no other reason than to say goodbye to Dennis.

On the final "Wiley" day, there was a similarly impressive turn out of ex-Wiley employees, including two previous Managing Directors, Ron Watson and Adrian Higham. The affection which everyone feels for Dennis was again clear in the effort that everyone made to be there.

Dennis was accompanied by his wife Maureen at all three

Staff and suppliers bid Dennis a fond farewell (1990)

parties, and he made full acknowledgement of her support over the years in his eloquent farewell speech (the part of the proceedings to which he had been looking forward least).

Dennis and Maureen are leaving for a round-the-world trip at the end of October; this is expected to last 5 months, and Dennis' many friends in Wiley contributed to his retirement present, new luggage for the trip.

When Dennis gets back from this holiday, he is planning to devote much of his time to lay church work in the parish of St Wilfred's in Chichester where he lives. It was to pursue this vocation that Dennis chose to take retirement at 60. He has, however, promised to make his expertise available to us on an occasional consultancy basis (and is already booked to help us next year with the new World Petroleum Congress).

All their many friends wish Dennis and Maureen a long and happy retirement together.

GOODWOOD BALL

On Friday 24th July 1987 the company held a ball at Goodwood House to celebrate 20 years of scientific publishing in Chichester. The beautiful setting helped to make it a very successful occasion,

Brad and Esto Wiley with Mr and Mrs Fritz Weg who came in 1962 when Interscience was bought by Wiley. Fritz's family owned the biggest scientific bookshop in Leipzig.

Peter and Diana Marriage (Peter was senior partner of Slaughter & May lawyers during the establishment of Wiley's European company)

Tricia Sharp (then Assistant Editor in the Biomedical programme) pictured at her retirement after many years at Wiley. Here she receives her leaving gift from Mike Dixon.

An important visitor to Wiley in 1991 was Mr Madron Seligman, our Euro-MP. Mr Seligman met all Directors and senior editorial and sales staff. He was here to discuss publishing opportunities in the EEC and plans for setting up an editorial office on the continent.

He is pictured here seated (centre) together with the Duke of Richmond (left), and the following Wiley staff listed by their then job titles: Mike Foyle, Managing Director (right) and standing, left to right, Mike Dixon, Publisher for Biomedical and Natural Science, Ernest Kirkwood, Publisher for Physical Sciences, John Jarvis, Publishing Director, Jim Dicks, Financial Director, Dawn Swarbrick, Personnel Manager, Bob Long, General Sales Manager and Mark Bide, Director of International Publishing Technology and Services.

Wiley Race Presentation. Left to right: W. Bradford Wiley II, Earlene Wiley, the couple from the syndicate owning "North Esk", the Duke of Richmond

The Paddock, Goodwood

which everyone enjoyed. Two of the people who were involved in the company from the outset—Jim Durrant and Mike Colenso—were present, as well as many pensioners such as Harry Newman, Thomas Traill and Senta Weg who remember the early days. Unfortunately, Ron Watson, the first Managing Director and his wife, Norah, were unable to be present. Mike Foyle gave a special welcome to the current members of staff who have been with the Company throughout the 20 years—Mike Coombs, David Pritchard, Dennis Fairs, Fred Rose, Peter Ferris and Marion Fisher.

Goodwood excelled itself with a magnificent buffet of roast turkey, honey-baked ham and Carrier duck salad. The tables were arranged throughout the state rooms and were beautifully decorated with flowers and candelabra. The evening was rounded off with dancing to the music of *Heritage* in a marquee erected in the grounds.

LONG SERVICE AWARDS

In May 1990 more than 60 people received long service awards for working at Wiley for 10 years or more. A buffet lunch was held at the Ship Hotel, where pink champagne was served on arrival. The awards were presented by Mike Foyle to those present who had served between 10 and 27 years each and nearly 1,000 years between them.

Long Service Awards—1990. From left to right: Marion Fisher, Renée Southwell, Irene Merry, Peggy Bradley, Mike Foyle, Karin Davies, Ove Steentoft, Peter Ferris and Monica Twine

Special Occasions 169

Peter Ferris and members of the Distribution Division—Long Service Awards

Christina Calzolari, Fé Naylor, Jackie Woodward

Anne Scott, Marion Fisher and Peggy Bradley

Long Service Awards—
(a) Martin Smart (journals production) and Carol Grainger (journals fulfilment)
(b) John Jarvis (editorial) and John Lea (marketing)
(c) Lynne Sullivan and Monica Twine (production)

Long Service Awards

Martin Smart and Carol Grainger receiving their awards from Mike Foyle

MICHAEL FOYLE RETIRES

John Jarvis (1992)

With this issue of *Grapevine* we mark the retirement of Michael Foyle on April 30th after thirty years with the company, the last ten of them as Managing Director.

Mike joined Wiley as European sales representative in 1963 when

Mike Foyle's retirement (1993)

"Now I'm retiring I shall have plenty of time to read!" Mike and Margaret at the Distribution Centre party to mark Mike's retirement.

The baton passes to John

the company was located in London, and only Peter Ferris and Mike Coombs remain of those who relocated with him to Chichester in 1967. The company then had 24 staff and made a net profit of £13,000, and Mike, by his own admission, had what was probably one of the most enviable jobs in publishing—representing a famous imprint, during the expansive 1960s, in some of the most amenable European locations.

As Sales and Marketing Director he enhanced the development of Chichester's own publishing programme, which transformed the company's profitability particularly following the Heyden journal acquisition in 1983 which coincided with his appointment as

Special Occasions 173

Julia Lampam (exhibitions, now publicity), Jonathan Agbenyega (editorial), Vanessa Lutman (editorial)

Eleanor Magilton (publishing), Rosemary Day (administration) and Shirley Howard (PA to Managing Director)

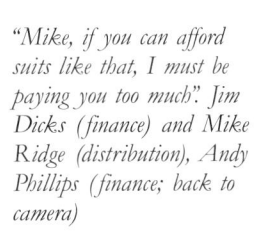

"Mike, if you can afford suits like that, I must be paying you too much". Jim Dicks (finance) and Mike Ridge (distribution), Andy Phillips (finance; back to camera)

MD. With his literary background and penchant for music and drama, his success as MD of a scientific publisher was not a foregone conclusion, yet under his leadership, the company has experienced its most successful years as we have grown in size and profitability to became a leader in our field.

During the March visit of the New York directors, I was pleased to have an opportunity to comment on Mike's retirement. I chose "style" as the enduring characteristic of his tenure which he used to create and sustain a unique atmosphere. In the last ten years, the publishing industry has witnessed deep recession, extreme currency fluctuations, technological revolution and rapacious conglomeration, but throughout all this Mike has kept our eyes firmly fixed on profitability as our key accountability to the Corporation, without once compromising opportunities or decent behaviour.

In the midst of this he (one of the most instinctive of managers) introduced a professional management programme to a recalcitrant, even cynical, workforce since he foresaw that our somewhat Corinthian attitude would not suffice in the harsher modern world. There are few now who doubt the improvements this programme has produced.

Throughout this entire period Mike has, of course, had the great good fortune to be partnered by his wife Margaret, who time will prove, has been an inimitable consort. As we offer Mike and Margaret our warmest wishes for a happy retirement, I am pleased to announce that Mike will remain on our Board as a non-executive director, and I have no doubt that he will quietly remind me of his legacy should things look like going awry in the future.

I feel privileged to have worked with Mike, and I know I thank him on behalf of the entire company for having brought us to our present enviable position.

CHAPTER TEN

Buildings

THE HISTORY OF WILEY'S EXPANSION INTO NEW BUILDINGS

View of the Corn Exchange before work commenced. All windows were made larger and the porch removed. The entrance to the building when occupied by Wiley can be seen on the extreme left.

View of the Corn Exchange before work commenced

Work starts

Ground floor of the Baffins Lane building in 1967

The reception in Baffins Lane in 1967

The board room in 1967

Baffins Lane building in the 1970s

The entrance to the Baffins Lane building

Buildings

The new Distribution Centre in the late 1960s. The warehouse area in the late 1960s and early 1970s was approximately 55,000 square feet, the floor space covering some 25,000 square feet. The remainder was occupied by bin and bulk storage racking. Fork lift trucks which could drive into containers were used in conjunction with two dock gates for loading or unloading. The total stock was 16,271 titles or 1,186,082 books. The Distribution Centre also housed the computer, customer service and book information departments.

The front entrance of the Distribution Centre

Harry Newman and Adrian Higham opening the new mezzanine floor at the Distribution Centre

The Booth Rooms building, before . . .

. . . And after

Stocklund House—first and second floors occupied by Production

CHAPTER ELEVEN

The Social Calendar

Wiley cricket team in the late 1970s. Back row: David Pritchard, Mike Foyle, Fred Rose, Martin Smart, Peter Ferris, Howard Jones. Front row: Andrew Foyle, Mike Pickering, Adrian Higham and unidentified player

JOHN WILEY CRICKET CLUB

Beginnings (Mike Shardlow, Senior Production Editor)

IN THE summer of 1973 cricket was in the air. A few bright sparks in John Wiley thought they could kindle the flame. Stuart Bell (Distribution Manager) and Mike Shardlow (Copy-editor) were playing for the same club at the weekend and were able to borrow the club's cricket gear for a midweek evening match. Fred Rose (Chief Draughtsman), through his local social contacts, was able to put us in touch with potential opponents and a match was arranged with MPA (now William Mercer). Stuart Bell undertook the booking of the Oaklands Park pitch through Chichester City Council, and Mike Shardlow undertook the mustering of the John Wiley forces. The match was played, and was a great success—for John Wiley. A return match was fixed up the same evening and two other matches against different opponents were played that summer. John Wiley won them all; this was an important factor in maintaining the enthusiasm of those whose willingness to play was vital to the enterprise. With some confidence in this enthusiasm, Mike Shardlow went ahead and booked a series of pitches for the summer of 1974, arranged opponents to play, and committed himself to the weekly task, in season, of raising eleven players from the staff and from the partners of staff. Through the good offices of Mike Foyle (Marketing Manager), the company committed itself too, to the extent of making sufficient money available to buy our own cricket gear. The Cricket Club was up and running.

REFLECTIONS

Martin Smart (Journals Production Manager)

It is my deep regret that I was not working for (and indeed had not even heard of) Wiley during the inaugural season of the cricket club. I remember speaking to Mike Shardlow shortly after I joined Wiley in late 1973 and getting excited about the prospect of donning "whites" again, after a gap of some ten years (since playing for my school).

We expanded the fixture list for that second season. I remember my first game: it was against Wingards at New Park Road. It was one of those games that cricketers hate. We batted first. I was number nine, I think. We started off assuredly, but soon began to stumble. Wickets fell. The light began to close in; rain threatened. We were 42 for 6. I was due in at the fall of the next wicket. I wanted to impress, but so did all the others in our team—and they had already perished! Rain started, slowly at first, then a steady stream. The opposition looked anxiously at the skies: we prayed for rain to save the game. The rain set in; the game was saved; everyone retired to the pub to talk about how things might have been.

And so my association with and fond memories of the club were forged. It's been hard: worrying about the fixtures; worrying about raising a side; then, on match days, worrying about the bloody weather! What a way to spend one's youth.

Over the years it has become somewhat more difficult to recruit players, particularly from within, and we've had to look more and more to outsiders to complete the team. Through my association with Lavant CC, I managed to obtain the loyal services of talented individuals such as Robin Burford, Ray Carter and Pat Emery (to name a few) to add to the likes of Dave Sparrow, Richard Stearn, Ben Woodrow and Ernie Ferrier, who originally had family members working at Wiley. This has helped us to achieve a competitive edge and to obtain generally good fixtures this past 24 years.

In 1997 we enter our 25th year, and have an excuse for a celebration! Our longevity is a measure of our success. We've had good seasons, and we've had bad seasons. Most important of all, it's been fun. We've had many a laugh, both on and off the field. And, best of all, we've got memories.

A COLLECTION OF MEMORIES

Mike Shardlow

An epigraph

Mrs Turner, of East Hoadley [sic], Sussex, wrote in a letter to a friend in 1739: "Last Munday my dear husband plaid at cricket & came home pleased anuf for he struck the best ball in the game and whisht he had not annything else to do he would play Cricket all his life."

This early match report is quoted in *Carr's Dictionary of Extraordinary English Cricketers* (J.L. Carr, Kettering, 1977).

A close finish

A close finish had been in prospect at Fishbourne Playing Field as John Wiley strove to reach and overtake their opponent's total. But it began to slip away from the batting side and, when they lost a wicket halfway through the last over, a win seemed out of the question. The next batsman comes in to join Pat Emery. Three balls left and 13 runs to win. The new batsman scrambles the ball away for a single to put Pat at the striking end. Two balls left and 12 runs to win. Statistically possible—but most unlikely. Pat hits the next ball, high and straight, onto the bowling green for six runs. Still statistically possible—but even more unlikely. Pat Emery's perfectly calm and confident exterior bespeaks a magisterial sense of purpose within himself. He shows no surprise when he hits the final ball of the match, high and long, back over the bowler and umpire till it comes to earth once again on the distant bowling green. But the crowd goes wild.

Dave Pritchard's XI

But then Dave Pritchard once hit 11 runs off the last ball. Mind you, we were batting first on this occasion so the result of the match didn't depend on it. It was down at Sidlesham, playing against Sidlesham and LSA (LSA?—the Land Settlement Association). We'd batted poorly through our 20 overs and scored far too few runs.

Anyway, it's the last ball of the last over. The bowler bowls.

Umpire: "No ball!"
Dave hits it for six.
The bowler delivers again.
Umpire: "No ball!"
Dave hits it for four.
With considerable circumspection the bowler bowls. The umpire remains silent. Dave scores a single off it.
One ball: 11 runs.

George Tackaberry

In the early years George Tackaberry was our scorer—our scorer and most ardent supporter. George was old; well beyond retirement age, he worked as a "post boy" at John Wiley. His fascinating working life had included touring, as a set designer, with Ivor Novello shows before the war. Now at John Wiley his strong social sensibility found its expression in the cricket team and the part he played in it. His small frame harboured powerful emotions and he exulted in our victories. He would be correspondingly bitter when our performance disappointed him. Then, like a wasp, he would harry us with his criticism, with his condemnation of our errors and our incompetence. And in the pub after the match, as we all reconciled our different views of the evening's events, he would be there with us, relishing his halves every bit as much as we relished our pints.

Pitched halfway between heaven and hell

We trooped into Her Majesty's Prison, Ford, on the evening of our very first visit there, with our eyes wide open to take in the strangeness of our surroundings. Once out on the field, the grassed-over former barrack square of what had been an RAF camp, we could look about us at the low prison buildings. To the north of the cricket pitch was the brick-built hall and other official or communal buildings. To the south were the rows of hut-buildings in which the prisoners lived.

Shortly after the game started, in a way that would become familiar in later seasons, the body of the prisoners swarmed out of the assembly they had to attend at 6p.m. and settled down round the field to watch the match. It wasn't just the number of spectators that took us aback and forced us to reassess our play as a performance, it was the sheer racket they made. The noisiest of the barrackers (and it was their own side that they barracked) were grouped at the southern end of the ground. No quarter was given; no allowance was made. Coarse language was used; rough oaths were bellowed out.

Struggling to overcome this distraction (and it was distraction we felt, not offence), we were, without warning, plunged into a sort of moral turmoil when the massed male voices of the prison choir rang out in roaring unison from the hall at the northern end of the ground. They were practising hymns for Sunday.

Caught in the middle of this surging, noisy, Miltonic battle between the voices of good and evil, we played out our game in a limbo of lightness and superficiality. We were astonished.

A brave start

It was a fairly rare occurrence for a new member of staff to respond with interest when approached about playing for the cricket team. So, when anyone did, there was always optimistic speculation amongst the older hands about his ability. Tony Llewellyn, tallish, well-built and reasonably athletic-looking, was a promising recruit. The first chance we had to look at him was in the 1985 season in the match against Amberley at their distant village ground in the pasture land beneath the Downs. The weather and the pitch were damp, and batting, as is often the case in such circumstances, was a dogged and grubby business. As a possible batsman, Tony was listed to bat at no. 5 or so, and his turn at the crease came after early batsmen had suffered and struggled to score any runs at all, and after they had lost their wickets in the attempt. Tony's first ball was shortish and straight. His bat described a swift arc and there was a ringing click. He had pulled the ball with incredible power and timing high over square leg. Still rising, the ball cleared the hedge on the boundary, carried right across the next field, high above the backs of the uncaring cattle, and dropped over the further hedge into the field beyond. He could not have made a more impressive start to an innings, or to a career with the team. You'd say it would be impossible to live up to. And so it proved.

Blood in the evening

Another evening up at the barracks the John Wiley team were struggling to make the target set for them by the Royal Military Police. There is not time, when you're batting in evening cricket, to try to take stock of the situation and play quietly. "Either get on with it or get out" is the brutalist philosophy of the evening game. At the crease we have a newcomer to the side, David Rosenberg (Editorial Director). He is plainly not a talented, or even a practised, batsman. We were glad enough to get him to play, but now we stand ungratefully in front of the pavilion, seething at his inactivity, sullenly wishing him out, for he is not scoring the runs we need.

Out in the middle the viewpoint is crucially different. David deploys what skill he has with the bat to defend his wicket. He can see no opportunity to plunder the attack for runs. He can only see that he has to prevent the opposition from getting him, getting John Wiley behind him, out. He shifts his grip so that his right hand is right down on the splice and brings considerable resources of concentration and determination to his task.

We grimly applaud him in at the end of the innings. We have lost; he remained undefeated.

People depart their various ways, get changed, go for a drink. Collecting up the kit and packing it away in the cricket bag we find that the batting glove David Rosenberg took off his right hand is soaked in blood. He had clearly taken one, perhaps many, severe blows from the ball and had split his thumb. David hardly played again and left the company, and the area, soon after.

Barring accidents, it takes several seasons for items of kit to wear out and be replaced. For several seasons the bloodstain on that glove, darkening with the years, was a reminder to us of the evening up at the military barracks where the stiff upper lip had been deployed and a sort of courage had been displayed. It was a reminder; it was also a reproach.

Information please

A cry you'll frequently hear at cricket grounds is: "Bowler's name, please?". It is the scorer. He sees the captain giving the ball to a fresh bowler and he wants to know what name to write in the scorebook before noting down the ball-by-ball details of the bowler's performance. The new bowler shouts his name back to the scorer and turns back to the business in hand.

At Ford prison one evening, John Wiley were batting, and the home skipper put a new bowler on to bowl. He wasn't just a new bowler, he was new to the prison and playing his first game for them. Who was he? Consternation buzzed among the prisoners gathered round the scorer's box. (It was just that, a large box, on wheels, like a tiny caravan, with a big window in the side that opened up for the scorer to look out of. It could be pulled around on its wheels and positioned anywhere it was wanted.) Well, the consternation resolved itself and a loud voice called across the ground to the players in the middle: "Bowler's crime, please?".

Harry Newman's catch

Harry Newman was older than the rest of us when we started to play cricket for John Wiley. But his nimble athleticism put many a young buck of a team-mate to shame. And he took plenty of wickets with his slow "wobblers". Up at Oaklands Park one evening John Wiley were in the field and I think our opponents were Ivanhoe. The ball was hit high to the midwicket boundary. Suddenly, there was Harry racing round to intercept it. At full speed, and travelling at right-angles to the flight of the ball, he stooped forward and caught the ball one-handed at knee level just inside the boundary. It was a world-class catch.

Making some play with the law about catches being not allowed when the fieldman is outside the boundary, but nonetheless getting it wrong, the umpire said, "Not out", and the batsman stayed at the crease. I don't remember the batsman now; but that was a good catch.

Corporal Allen makes an impression

It is the nature of army life that soldiers move about a lot from one posting to another. So though we played against the Royal Military Police at the Roussillon Barracks every year, we rarely saw the same player twice. We hadn't seen Corporal Allen before, for instance, when he came out to open the innings for them one evening, in the late 1970s it must have been. He did make quite a big physical impression, though, on our routinely curious eyes. He had the body, and particularly the neck, of an international prop forward. Moving swiftly for so big a man, as they say, he battered the first ball straight back at the bowler so hard that he couldn't get out of the way and it hit him—fortunately somewhere that could recover from it.

The routinely curious eyes of those of us fielding in front of the bat hooded over on receipt of this information, and we surreptitiously shrank back several yards before the next ball came to be bowled.

A confrontation

Confrontations are the nub of cricket. But picture Robin Burford, captain of the John Wiley team for several seasons. He's 5 foot 7 inches, slender, pale, bespectacled. He is clipping the bowling away for runs behind square on the offside. Now picture the bowler: an increasingly irritated and increasingly aggressive county second eleven fast bowler (it's true what they say, you get all sorts in prison—we're at Ford again). He's of West Indian origin, nephew of a legendary West Indian test cricketer; he's tall and powerfully built and not cool, not at all cool, but impetuous and scary.

The bowling becomes even faster, and now somewhat short-pitched. Of course, you're trapped at the crease. There is nowhere to go. Just keep your eyes wide open and watch out for yourself. Robin admitted afterwards that he was just trying to make himself inconspicuous, really; rather regretted scoring the runs in fact; only made things worse. But, oh, the glory!

Fig. 1. This report of John Wiley's very first cricket match appeared in the Chichester Observer in August 1973. Three further matches were played that season. One of them was a return match against MPA, which we also won. Under the various names the firm adopted, MPA remained regular opponents until their team folded in 1996. Dave Pritchard's 72 not out was the highest score by any John Wiley player for two decades. The present record is the century scored in Priory Park against Midland Bank by Richard Stearn.

Wiley & Sons v. M.P.A.

On a fine evening at Oaklands Park last Monday, John Wiley emerged clear victors in their first match, beating M.P.A. by 40 runs. Batting first, Wiley's Bell and Pritchard put on 28 for the first wicket before Bell, striking out, was bowled. Pritchard remained, scoring freely, to prop up the innings and came in with a fine undefeated 72, which included two sixes and four fours. None of the other batsmen made much of a show and Wiley totalled 111 for eight.

M.P.A.'s early batsmen were immediately in trouble against the quickish bowling of Chamberlain and Shardlow, three wickets falling for eight runs in the first six overs.

Wickets continued to fall until Dixon (30) and Briggs (7) came together in a stand of 32 for the eighth wicket. This partnership was broken by Rose, bowling very accurately. Only Dixon, defending staunchly, now stood between Wiley and victory, but he finally succumbed to a slower ball from Shardlow.

John Wiley 111—8 (Pritchard 72 n.o., Bell 22; Dixon 3—10, Shepherd 2—22, Banks 2—30). M.P.A. 71 (Dixon 30, Stemp 10, extras 19; Chamberlain 4—7, Shardlow 3—3, Rose 2—7).

John Wiley v. Sidlesham

An exhilarating, high-scoring draw, made possible by the trueness of the New Park Road wicket, was the result of John Wiley's game against Sidlesham on Wednesday.

Runs flowed freely from the bat all evening. Rogers and Hickman opened for John Wiley and had 93 on the board before being separated. Chaplin, Sparrow and Foyle all got in among the runs immediately upon arrival at the crease, and the John Wiley innings closed at 150 for three.

Sidlesham announced their intention of overhauling this formidable total by scoring 12 runs off the first over of their innings. Richardson, Johnson and Jupp would brook no containment and the score galloped along.

The fall of wickets brought less forceful batsmen to the crease, though, and the run rate began to falter in the closing overs.

Smith, bowling a level-headed, accurate medium-pace, and some tight fielding, meant that Sidlesham required three runs to win off the last over. Smith clean bowled two batsmen with his first and third balls and it was still three runs to win with one ball left.

The batsmen completed two runs from an off-drive so the game ended with the scores level to the amazement and delight of everyone involved.

John Wiley 150-3 (Hickman 66, Rogers 34, Chaplin 28 n.o., Sparrow 15).

Sidlesham 150-3 (Johnson 91 n.o., Jupp 28, Richardson 12).

Fig. 2. A report (from the Chichester Observer, July 1976) tells all about our famous level-score draw with Sidlesham. This was the long, hot summer that broke all records. There was generally a glut of runs in local cricket.

John Wiley v M.P.A.

Rose's excellent opening spell shattered the M.P.A. early batting; he took four wickets for three runs in his first three overs. But Stemp, who survived this onslaught, and Millyard batted with skill to regain the initiative, putting on 40 runs together.

It was Hickman with his off-spin who not only broke this partnership but took two more wickets in the same over to redress the balance for the fielding side.

Facing the modest total of 90, John Wiley found themselves struggling as Dixon and Millyard struck early blows for M.P.A. Chaplin played several fine shots at number five to give John Wiley some hope but, despite a brave effort by Smart at number nine, Lamb in a meritorious display of accurate aggressive bowling saw to it that John Wiley were dismissed without reaching their target.

M.P.A. 90-9 (Stemp 35 n.o., Millyard 22, Lamb 12; Rose 4-12, Hickman 3-16, Smart 1-10).

John Wiley 71 (Chaplin 21, Smart 11 n.o., Rogers 10; Lamb 5-7, Millyard 2-19, Dixon 2-21). 15/8/75

Fig. 3. A report from the Chichester Observer in August 1975 of our match against MPA. The fact that they beat us shows that we no longer trample ever-triumphant over our opponents as we did in 1973.

C.O Mercer Fraser
23/7/87 v. John Wiley

Croydon and Davies put on 37 for third wicket for Mercer Fraser. After tight bowling by Rose the side ended at 99 for five.

John Wiley started poorly and were only 21 for two after seven overs. But Woodrow and Burford scored 79 off the next five overs as the Mercer Fraser bowling and fielding deteriorated. Woodrow's innings of 46 included eight fours and a six.

John Wiley won with seven overs to spare in very poor light.

MERCER FRASER
Croydon b Shardlow	26
Stewart c Sparrow b Carter	12
Bailey lbw b Rose	0
Davies b Russell	32
Hazelden b Shardlow	0
Johnson not out	13
Hine not out	1
Extras	15
Total (for 5 wkts)	99

Fall of wickets: 1-32, 2-32, 3-69, 4-69, 5-89.
Bowling: Rose 1-12, Carter 1-22, Russell 1-32, Shardlow 2-33.

JOHN WILEY
Stearn run out	5
Russell b Rowntree	0
Sparrow b Hirons	39
Woodrow not out	46
Burford not out	14
Extras	6
Total (for 3 wkts)	100

Fall of wickets: 1-6, 2-20, 3-50.
Bowling: Shepherd 1-29, Rowntree 1-9.

Fig. 4. Mercer Fraser (MPA as was) wrote this report for the Chichester Observer in July 1987. John Wiley are back in winning form over their old opponents and Mercer Fraser permit themselves a brief whinge about the poor light, which is a perennial difficulty that evening cricketers have to contend with.

John Wiley v. Mercer Fraser

John Wiley batted first on an unpredictable wicket. They reached a total of 79 with Garfield (33) top scoring and Woodrow (11) the only other in double figures. Five of the wickets were taken for 20 runs by Matthews.

With the light diminishing, Mercers chased the runs. Their openers fell cheaply and it was Reeves, seen for the first time without sunhat, who controlled the innings (42 not out). They lost only six wickets in their chase for the total and with a four from Reeves brought up the winning score of 83. Smart took three wickets for 15 runs.

JOHN WILEY
Stearn b Matthews	2
Burford c, b Malcolm	1
Woodrow b Malcolm	11
Sparrow b Matthews	8
Usansky c, b Mathews	5
Wilson b Malcolm	0
Rose b Matthews	1
Garfield c, b Bailey	33
Smart b Matthews	0
Russell c, b Bailey	3
Carter not out	2
Extras	13
Total	79

Bowling: Matthews 5-20; Malcolm 3-12.

MERCER FRASER
Croydon c, b Smart	4
Stewart b Smart	5
Stemp c, b Smart	1
Reeves not out	42
Davies b Rose	1
Stoakes b Carter	12
Bailey c, b Carter	4
Smith not out	1
Extras	13
Total (6 wkts)	83

Bowling: Smart 3-15; Carter 2-11.

Fig. 5. The report, from the Chichester Observer in August 1988, of the match against Mercer Fraser. All eleven John Wiley players' names are listed, providing a snapshot of a typical team of that era.

```
                    JOHN WILEY C.C.    1975 SEASON

            Played   14     Won  6    Lost  8

                             AVERAGES

BATTING (Qualification: 2 completed innings)
            Innings   Not out   Runs   Average
Foyle          6         1       184    36.8
Sparrow       11         3       212    26.5
Shardlow       8         4       101    25.3
Rogers        11         3       195    24.4
Smart          6         3        39    13.0
Hickman        4         0        43    10.8
Pritchard     11         1       100    10.0
Newman        10         2        57     7.1
Bird           9         1        55     6.9
Pickering      8         0        50     6.3
Jeavons        3         0        17     5.7
Rose           4         0        17     4.3
Twine          2         0         5     2.5
Ferris         3         1         6     2.0
Williams       4         0         7     1.8

Also batted: Smith 13, 0 n.o., 0 n.o.;   Gard 12, 29 n.o.;
    Warrington 24;  Chaplin 21;  Barnett 14;  Trayler 11;
    Bell 4;  P.Smart 4;  Fox 1 n.o.;  Watt 1.

Fifties:  Foyle      57 n.o.   v.  Royal Military Police
          Shardlow   57 n.o.   v.  County Hall
          Rogers     51 n.o.   v.  Ivanhoe

BOWLING
            Overs   Maidens   Runs   Wickets   Average
Rose        38.4       4       153     16        9.6
Hickman     15         2        76      7       10.9
Rogers       6         0        45      4       11.6
Shardlow    57.3       5       201     16       12.6
Sparrow     45         3       188     12       15.7
Smart       21.3       0       156      9       17.3
Foyle       11         0        54      3       18.0
Pritchard   15.4       1        90      3       30.0
Smith        7         0        44      1       44.0
Trayler      9         0        47      1       47.0
Ferris       4         0        48      1       48.0
Newman       7         1        50      1       50.0

Also bowled: Pickering 2-0-6-0;   Bell 3-0-12-0;   Fox 2-0-13-0;
    Gard 2-0-13-0;  Watt 5-0-16-0;  Acres 1-0-19-0; Warrington 6-0-32-0.

FIELDING:    Stumpings: 1 each by Chaplin, Pritchard and P. Smart.
             Catches: 5--Rogers;     3--Bird, Foyle, Newman, Sparrow;
                      2--Pickering, Shardlow;
                      1--Bell, Chaplin, Fox, Hickman, Rose, Smart, Smith.
```

Fig. 6. The 1975 averages, carefully compiled from the scorebook at the end of the season. Mike Foyle enjoys prime position at the top of the batting averages. Superbly stylish, his left-handed batting was beyond emulation by the rest of us—evidence of what must have been his well-spent youth.

```
                John Wiley & Sons Cricket Team
                   Batting & Bowling Analysis
                           1985 Season

                   Played 15   Won 4   Lost 11

 Batting*        Matches   Innings   Not Out   Runs    Average

 A. Llewellyn       6         6         2       176     44.0
 R. Stearn         13        13         2       278     25.3
 R. Carter          3         3         2        20     20.0
 R. Burford        14        14         1       238     18.3
 M. Shardlow       11         9         3       104     17.3
 B. Woodrow        13        13                 148     11.4
 I. Shelley        14        12         1       121     11.0
 S. Usansky         5         3         1        20     10.0
 D. Sparrow        13        12                 109      9.1
 K. Garfield       14        10         3        45      6.4
 J. Wilson         14         9         4        21      4.2
 P. Smart           6         6         1        20      4.0
 F. Rose           10         2                   7      3.5
 P. Kisray          4         4                   6      1.5

 Extras                                         116
 Total                                          1253
 **Qualification: 2 completed Innings

                           Fifties

 A. Llewellyn          62 Not Out    V Midland Bank
 R. Stearn             51 Not Out    V Shippams

                      Bowling Analysis

                                                        Runs
                 Overs   Maidens   Runs   Wickets  Average  per over
 M. Shardlow     52.4      4       199      17      11.71    3.78
 D. Sparrow      34.2      2       195      15      13.00    5.68
 J. Wilson        8.2      0        47       3      15.67    5.64
 D. Pritchard    17.2      0       127       8      15.88    7.33
 R. Burford      12        1        95       5      19.00    7.92
 M. Smart        20.1      0        97       5      19.40    4.81
 F. Rose         54        5       273      12      22.75    5.06
 A. Llewellyn    22        0       156       6      26.00    7.09
 R. Stearn       17.3      0       145       5      29.00    8.29
 R. Carter       19        0       112       2      56.00    5.89
 G. Smith         9        0        83       0               9.22

                           Catches

 Stearn    7      Burford  4      Shardlow  3      M. Smart   2
                  Shelley  4      P. Smart  2      Woodrow    2
                  Kisray   2      Garfield  2      Sparrow    2
                  Wilson          Usansky          Carter     Rose   Burford
```

Fig. 7. The averages for the 1985 season. Ten years on from Fig. 6, many, but not all, of the names have changed.

1984 John Wiley CRICKET CLUB

Date	Opponents	Ground	Start
Thurs 3 May	RMP	Barracks	6.00
Thurs 10 May	Ivanhoe	Oaklands	6.00
Tues 15 May	Wingards	New Park Road	6.00
Thurs 24 May	Lavant	New Park Road	6.00
Thurs 31 May	Ashling	New Park Road	6.00
Tues 5 June	Bishop Otter College	College, Chichester	6.00
Thurs 14 June	Natwest Bank	New Park Road	6.00
Wed 20 June	Francis Parker	Oaklands	6.00
Mon 25 June	Midland Bank	New Park Road	6.00
Fri 6 July	Shippams	New Park Road	6.00
Tues 10 July	Harris & Porter	New Park Road	6.00
Thurs 19 July	MPA	New Park Road	6.00
Thurs 26 July	Ford Prison	Ford	6.00
Thurs 2 Aug	Portsmouth Social Services	New Park Road	5.45
Wed 8 Aug	Rowes Garage	Oaklands	5.45
Wed 15 Aug	Dave Pritchard's XI	Pagham C.C.	5.30

Fig. 8. Fred Rose designed this atmospheric fixtures list for 1984 to replace the more utilitarian model previously put out. The list shows the wide range of companies, institutions and villages that John Wiley played over the years.

JOHN WILEY CRICKET CLUB 1987
FIXTURE LIST

Date	Opponent	Venue	Time
Thurs 7 May	Lavant	New Park Road	6.00
Thurs 14 May	Harris & Porter	New Park Road	6.00
Thurs 21 May	Schoolmasters	Boys' High School	6.00
Thurs 28 May	Amberley	Amberley	6.00
Thurs 4 June	Midland Bank	New Park Road	6.00
Thurs 11 June	Shippams	New Park Road	6.00
Thurs 18 June	RMPs	Barracks	6.00
Wed 24 June	Ford Prison	Ford Prison	6.00
Sat 4 July	Henry Ling	Dorchester	2.30
Thurs 9 July	Spire Print	New Park Road	6.00
Wed 15 July	MPA	New Park Road	6.00
Thurs 23 July	Wingards	New Park Road	6.00
Wed 29 July	Natwest Bank (Away)	to be confirmed	6.00
Wed 5 Aug	Ashling	Ashling	5.45
Wed 12 Aug	Dave Pritchard's XI	Pagham	5.45

Nil Disputandum
(No Room For Argument)

Fig. 9. Fred Rose's even more atmospheric and lively design for the 1987 fixtures list. In July two matches are scheduled against suppliers (of typesetting and printing). Such matches, arranged "within the trade", have been an occasional rather than a regular feature of the fixtures.

Christmas 1967—Doug Mason and Mike Colenso, 2nd and 3rd from left

Marion Fisher and Mike Coombs among the revellers

Christmas 1967—Ron Watson (centre) and Dennis Fairs on his right

David Pritchard (far right)

A Marketing party in the late 1980s
Left: Julie Morgan
Below: Steve Sidaway

Left: Lyn Udall
Below: Belinda Griffiths and Jane Southwell

The Editorial Christmas lunch 1990

Above: Mike Davis checking whether Mike Dixon is done to a turn

Right: Mike Dixon

Below: "The party popper didn't work"—Verity Waite

Two memorable characters both of whom left in 1987

Tony Llewellyn (General Marketing Manager)

Peter Shepherd, Publisher, Physical Sciences (left)

202   *Thirty Years in Chichester: A Celebration*

Customer Service summer outing 1994 to Dell Quay

Before—Rachel Robinson . . .

. . . and after—Diana Butterly, Jacque Allen, Thelma Watson, Matthew Collins' legs, Jenny James

*Belinda Giacopazzi and
Sarah Mason*

*The proof is in the
pudding—Karin Davies*

Above: Lager louts—Production summer trip to France (1990)

Right: Actually it's Goodwood, but they look good enough for Royal Ascot—(Production outing 1985)

Below: Admin summer trip to Windsor 1989 or 1990

"Give me a fix, Mr Navigator"
Production Department Biddles Christmas Party,
HMS Belfast—1989

Cor, what a cracker!
Janine Toole, Christmas 1988

Editorial Department—"The Heavenly Choir"

206 *Thirty Years in Chichester: A Celebration*

Editorial Summer outings, 1990

Wiley carnival float, Chichester 1982. The Wise Owl *was constructed in the Order Processing office—after office hours, of course.*

The first ten years—Goodwood House 1977.

The second company-wide picnic day, Goodwood 1996

Cheering the tug of war teams—Goodwood, 1996

Gordon Barclay was trying so hard, they deserved to win

CHAPTER TWELVE

Memorable Communications

Copy of this letter sent to the NATIONAL ACADEMY OF SCIENCES (Washington)

John WILEY & Sons Limited
Baffins Lane
CHICHESTER
West Sussex
England.

Dear Mr. Southward,

PAPER: MATHEMATICAL FORMULATION OF THE CLUTCHING

I have received your letter of the January 4, 1989, with encl. 2 my letters (December 30, 1987 and November 2, 1988).

I am much surprised and vexed at having returned to me the letters. When Academy found not in position to publish my theory, the Academy should have advised me of the fact, putting me to the greatest inconvenience. What about a strong moral sense ?

As my theory and ALL documents sent are MY OWN PROPRIETY, please return:
1°- My article "MATHEMATICAL FORMULATION OF THE CLUTCHING";
2°- Practical annex "TOUT-KOWSKY'S METHOD OF CLUTCH EVALUATION SEQUENCE" for quick GRAPHIC determination;
3°- Figures 1, 1' (prime), 2, 3 and 4;
4°- A leaflet entitled "A GUIDE TO THE SELECTION OF CLUTCHES";
5°- A leaflet "INERTIAS".

Yours sincerely,

Dear Flavour and Fragrance Journal

Please send me information on your publication, if possible, please. I admire the art of perfume making and wish to market some of my own. Also to collect and inventory. I am one of those people, like Andy Warhol, who would like a museum of fragrance permanent building and staff.

However, I envision new paths in perfumerie, untrodden as yet. I can't get along with less that 100 perfumes. My memory for fragrances is amazing. I smell everything like a dog. I remember smelling the Alain

Delon men's cologne 15 years ago or so and thinking, "finally – _real_ fragrance for men"! I was moved beyond words by his attempt to free men from horrors like "Brut" and "Aramis," and lately "TSAR," even worse!

Well, hoping to hear from you soon. Thank you.

Sincerely,
Melissa Pride

Homicide Psychic Investigation

P.S. You could send an old copy of your publication if you wish, I have never seen it, or just subscription forms.

湖北省化学研究所

中国海关：

　　我所李小定同志的《利用XRF研究玻璃中的铜的价数》一文已被国际杂志《X射线光谱》录用。这是该篇论文的校样稿。

　　经审查，无泄密等问题，请予放行。

致

礼！

湖北省化学研究所
1990.2.10.

地址：武昌关山鲁家巷　电话：八七〇四二三　八七〇四二四　电报挂号

This one arrived without a translation . . .

Memorable Communications

COMPUTER SIMULATION OF SALAMI DRYING

L IMRE AND T. KÖRNYEY

Technical University Budapest, 1521 Budapest, Hungary

SUMMARY

Salami sorts are made of special meat pastes filled in hygroscopic casing and preserved by drying.

The characteristic features and the time of drying are greatly affected by the operational conditions.

Factories are interested in reducing the time of the drying treatment. To determine a reliable and economic drying schedule a physical-mathematical model has been elaborated and used. The system of equations has been solved numerically by using the FDM technique for the determination of the temperature, concentration and stress fields as a function of the time. Computed results have been verified by experiments.

By the numerical analysis it has been proved that the maximum rate of drying to be permitted is limited by the danger of possible deformation and inner fissures caused by tensile stresses occurring if shrinkage is prevented.

On the basis of the proper drying schedule an algorithm and a strategy of the microprocessing operational control has been elaborated.

ACKNOWLEDGEMENTS

This research has been supported by University of Mining and Metallurgy grant 11.120.15 and Frontier Research Program, Artificial Brian Systems Laboratory, RIKEN, ~~Tokyo~~, Japan [Wako-shi]

Mr. Baffine Lane
Journals Production
John Wiley & Sons Ltd
Chichester
Sussex PO19 1UD
UK

Dear Mr. Lane:

Please find enclosed the "Original Figures for Paper No 2237/1910" :

      The h-p Version of the Finite Element Method
          for Problems with Interfaces

> Dear Dr Baffins Lane.
>
> I am returning the corrected proofs for our paper together with the reprint order form, in which I have requested 125 reprints including 25 free copies.

To
JOURNAL PRODUCTION DEPARTMENT
JOHN WILEY AND SONS LIMITED
U.K.

Dear Sir,

    Thank you very much for the set of the proofs which corrections are being sent to you. I look forward to have cooperation from your end. Thank you again for your kind c

    Thanking with regards,

        Sciencerely Your's

A lot of thanks the people from printer's group who help us the article look correct.

    Yours sincerely

        authors

John Wiley & Sons Limited
Baffins Lane, Chichester, West Sussex, England, PO19 1UD.

```
Professor Dr-Ing Heinz Duddeck
Telefon 05 31/6 32 47
Greifswaldstrabe 38
3300 Braunschweig
FEDERAL REPUBLIC OF CHINA


Waybill No: JP 0646/3   NAG 578
```

Acknowledgements

We would like to thank Dr. D. Kaesermann, University of Bern, for the kind supply of the BO samples and Dr. F. Huber, University of Bern, for the generous gift of the three subunits IIAB^{Man}, IIC^{Man} and IID^{Man} of the mannose transporter complex.

```
Mrs. C. Chaplin
c/o John   Wiley&Sons Ltd
Beffins Lane
CHICHESTER, Sussex PO19 1 UD
ENGLAND
```

Dear Mrs. Chaplin

this is a flower bouquet for you.

Thanks for your kind letter from 17 March.

```
Mrs. Fernanda Naylor
c/0 WILEY
Baffins Lane
CHICHESTER,West Sussex
PO19  1UD
 GB
```

My dear Fernanda,

I had an ugöy"chinese"flu for almost a whole month.

First I must thank you for the nice picture of a young lady about 32 . Meanwhile I passed the 75....

 Please do what you think is good(review to rev.Manager).

Now I must tell you something: Wiley had a booth at an exhibition in Munich last year, but I don not know which. There were two very young ladies from Chichester. They did not know a single name from all those I know. What a big bee's hive must be Wiley - and all ladies. The few gents what do they do ???
Perhaps this is the reason why England cant follow the German industrial peak ?
The only thing the Birith have,is money to buy land in Munich and elsewhere (Murdoch !)

As I do not know how long I live I would be happy to have royalties before I leave this unjust earth. Could you please call the lady in charge
The next time I am in England you will be the reason that I visit Wiley.

Cordially

Customer Services

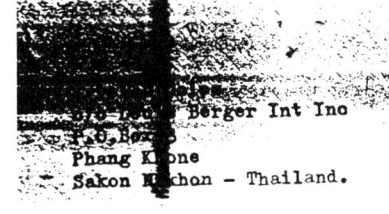

28th March 1981

Berger Int Inc
P.O. Box
Phang Khone
Sakon Nakhon – Thailand.

Messrs John Wiley & Sons Ltd.   Att. Miss P Smylie
Disribution Cenrte
Southern Cross Trading Estate
1 oldlands Way
Bognor Regis
West Sussex PO22 9SA

Dear Miss Smylie

I have recieved both parcels of books, one arrived by surface mail and the other by airmail – the last sent off. BUT – all the books were covered in what I take to be jam, just a ----*** sticky mess. So, I will not return them to you, neither is the local post office responcible for the situation, however, a Thai colleague has taken them over from me so all is well. I only hope that the person sending jam by post will know better now that her prize jam has landed up in the wastepaper basket.

I am requesting my bank to send you the sum of £75.75 to cover the cost of these books. I am sorry to have caused you any inconvenience.

Yours sincerely

Erroll D Coles

Dear Sir,

The brightness of this day has given me the great opportunity to write you this Letter. Before I go on with my words may GOd the giver of all good things bless your success.

Sir, I beg you in the name of God to send me other shoe or tea shirt or every thing you need (wont) to give me. and I am sure that you can give me one of what I have said.

Yours in Christ

David Okyere

WEPF & CO. BASEL
Schweiz Suisse Switzerland

BUCHHANDLUNG
ANTIQUARIAT / VERLAG
Telephon: (061) 25 63 77 (Antiquariat: 25 63 79)

BOOKSELLERS
LIBRAIRES / EDITEURS
Telex 62 027 / Telegramme: Wepfco Basel / Postcheck 40-226

[signature]

John Wiley & Sons Ltd.
Southern Cross Trading Estate
Shripney Rd.
Bognor Regis, W.Sussex, PO22 9SA
England

Ihr Zeichen:
Unser Zeichen: us-ff 0114

CH-4001 BASEL, 16.2.1981
Eisengasse 5 (bei der Mittleren Rheinbrücke)

~~REQUEST TO~~ RETURN

Quant.	Invoice No. and Date	Author, Title	Netprice
1	51508/3.2.81	Temple, The Chemistry of Heterocyclic Compounds, Vol. 37 Triazoles 1,2,4	149.60 U.S.Dollars

The edge of the back-cover was gnawed by mice.

Please exchange immediately

20/2
1

Post

1

Amsterdam, 8th May 1981

Hello again,

Because Lulu is on holiday in Greece I have the honour to order something. Here we go :

10	0471 08124-8	8080/Z80 Assembly Language Language (Miller)
3	0471 27835-1	PASCAL: The Language and its implementation
2	?	ATARI Basic Selfteaching guide

That's it. You see, a small order only for Wiley books because we have got other suppliers for Hayden books.

The reason why we can not order Hayden books from you are :
- High prices
- Small discounts
- Extravagant transport charges

I am sorry about all because the service is quite right.

Cheers

Frans de Vreeze

Afterword

John Jarvis (Managing Director)

THE SENTIMENTS expressed in these pages go some way to describing what has been achieved in Chichester over the last 30 years, and also provide some explanation of what has made Wiley so successful during that time.

It is an interesting coincidence that at the same time as the conception of this volume, the corporation established a group of senior managers to consider the relative roles of subsidiary and parent companies within an international or global enterprise such as Wiley. It is possible that this group might suggest that the very terms "parent" and "subsidiary" may be outmoded, and that the truly global company is better characterised as geographically distributed centres of expertise. All enterprises need an HQ and the location of Wiley's is clear. But it is also clear that a company may employ a single representative in a particular territory, or support the development of a local publishing operation in the anticipation that these initiatives can generate business in these locations more efficiently than HQ could working from a distance.

The Wiley company that moved to Chichester 30 years ago was still primarily involved in selling Wiley's US copyrights throughout its markets, but even then an embryonic publishing programme consisting of UK and continental European copyrights was in existence, and it has grown steadily to become a major revenue and profit provider.

Wiley has always been renowned for the quality of its book publishing, but the Chichester story would be incomplete if we failed to record the significance of the journals. These unique, serial publications which act as vehicles for the dissemination of primary research findings have afforded beneficial financial returns to many publishers over the past 30 years and although Wiley was a little slow to benefit in the early years, we have certainly caught up fast. The acquisition of Interscience Publishers in the 1960s, with

John Jarvis with Executive Board Members and new Wiley-VCH Managing Director, Dr Manfred Antoni. From left to right: Angela Poulter (HR Director), Manfred Antoni, John Jarvis, Steven Mair (Publishing Director), Peter Ferris (IT and Customer Service Director), Bob Long (Sales & Marketing Director) and Jim Dicks (Financial Director).

its European origins, established our journal presence and further acquisitions of Heyden & Sons Ltd (1983), Alan R Liss Inc. (1989), and most recently VCH (1996) have brought us amongst the leading journal players. These acquisitions provided momentum but, all the while, indigenous development of the journal programme was occurring in New York and Chichester.

It is impossible to mention everyone involved in this development, because it was in fact the entire company, but we must gratefully remember Jamie Cameron and his editorial vision, and also past colleagues such as Brenda Flooks (journal fulfilment) and Jim Painter (journal production)—all professionals who established the basis of the journal business we enjoy today.

My own background was in journal publishing at Elsevier and I am grateful to Mike Foyle, among others, for backing the continuing development of our journals over the last 10 years, during which time we have begun to come to terms with the radical technological changes about to transform journal publishing as we have known it. As with all change we at first deny it, then resist it, but eventually embrace it and, as a company, we are now well into this third phase.

The essential insight I have gained from these recollections is that while it is improbable that Wiley in Chichester has always been blessed with the best people in the industry, we have had our disproportionate share of people who have given us their best, year in and year out. That, to me, is an even greater testimony to the past and legacy for the future.

In 1988 ...
New York journal subscriptions fulfilment transfers to UK

Sales exceed £20 million (FY88)

Will Pesce joins Wiley Inc. as head of College Division

Wiley Ltd takes over responsibility for Japanese market

John Wilde leaves the company

The 1990s
Wiley Inc. acquires Alan R. Liss publishers

US Board of Directors meet in UK for the first time in 1990

Charles Ellis succeeds Ruth McMullin as President and Chief Executive Officer of Wiley Inc. (1990)

Bob Long becomes Sales & Marketing Director

Tim Davies leaves to join Pergamon Press

    Margaret Thatcher resigns as Prime Minister in 1990

Joint venture with Nauka in Moscow established

Jim Dicks joins as Financial Director (1991)

John Wilson leaves to be Marketing Director for Prentice Hall

Wiley Ltd acquires Chancery Law

New offices opened in Strasbourg and Paris

Sales exceed £25 million (FY90)

John Jarvis succeeds Mike Foyle as Managing Director of Wiley Europe (1993)

Michael Dixon is appointed Editorial Director

Sales exceed £30 million (FY93)

Brad Wiley II takes over as Chairman of John Wiley & Sons Inc.

Steven Mair joins as Director of Professional Publishing

Wiley Ltd acquires Belhaven Press

Sales exceed £35 million (FY94)

In 1995 ...
Angela Poulter joins the company as Human Resource Manager

Wiley Europe launches its first journal on the Internet (*E J Theoretical Chemistry*)

West Street offices are opened for Professional and IT